NEXT MOVE

MOVE

WORKBOOK

WITH MP3 CD

3

JOE McKENNA

Contents

Starter Unit

Grammar and Vocabulary

to be

1   Complete the conversations with the correct form of *to be*.

   1 A *Is* Emma your sister?
   B No, she *isn't*.
   2 A Where .... you from?
   B I .... from Sweden.
   3 A How old .... your parents?
   B Dad .... 38 and Mum .... 34.
   4 A .... there any cafés near here?
   B Yes, there .... one around the corner.

have got

2   Match the questions (1–5) to the answers (a–e). Then complete the answers with the correct form of *have*.

   1 Have you got any pets?   *d*
   2 Has Jared got a sister?
   3 Have your parents got a car?
   4 Has Bethany got red hair?
   5 Have we got time for a sandwich?

   a No, she .... Her hair's brown.
   b Yes, we .... Class starts in fifteen minutes.
   c Yes, they .... It's a big family car.
   d No, I *haven't*. I don't like animals.
   e Yes, he .... Her name's Andrea.

be and *have got*

3   Choose the correct options.

   1 Tamara *is* / *has got* 16 years old.
   2 My cousins *are* / *have got* a big house.
   3 Sorry, I *'m not* / *haven't got* time to talk right now.
   4 Sara's boyfriend *is* / *has got* very tall.
   5 Kevin *is* / *has got* long brown hair.
   6 My grandparents *are* / *have got* very active.
   7 We *aren't* / *haven't got* much money.
   8 Their flat *isn't* / *hasn't got* very new.

Possessive *'s*

4   Look at the picture and complete the sentences with *'s* or *s'*.

We're the Russell family. Our parents Cathy and Matt have got three children. The [1] children*'s* names are Ben, Laura and Phil. (That's me, Laura in the middle!) That's [2] Mum .... car, and you can also see [3] Dad .... bicycle. We have got three dogs. The [4] dog .... names are Fido, Blackie and Moonie. That's our [5] family .... house behind them. We live at number 34, and our neighbours the Watsons live at number 36. Our dogs often run after the [6] Watson .... cat. Their [7] cat .... name is Smoky.

is, *has* and possessive *'s*

5   Read the conversation. Look at the *'s*. Write *is*, *has* or possessive.

   A What**'s** your surname?   [1] *is*
   B It**'s** Kennedy. That**'s** got two Ns.
   [2] ....   [3] ....
   A My aunt**'s** name**'s** Kennedy too! Where**'s** the name from?   [4] ....
   [5] ....   [6] ....
   B My father says it**'s** from Ireland.
   [7] ....

Subject and object pronouns

6 **Complete the sentences with the correct pronouns.**

1 I'm going shopping. Do *you* want to come with *me*?

2 Stella's upstairs. ....'ll come down in a moment, and then you can talk to ....

3 Tom's working. ....'ll come home at two o'clock and ....'ll have lunch together.

4 Are the children outside? Can you ask .... to come inside? .... need to have a bath.

5 We've got a letter from Brian! .... always writes to .... in the summer.

Possessive adjectives

7 **Complete the sentences with the correct possessive adjectives.**

1 We're from Japan. *Our* names are Yumi and Keiko.

2 He's the manager. .... car's parked at the front door.

3 I'm the new teacher. It's .... job to help you speak English.

4 That's Barry's bike. .... frame is made of aluminium.

5 She's a cyclist. .... name's Yadida.

Common verbs

8 **Put the letters in the correct order to complete the text.**

Today we're reporting from our summer camp. There are lots of activities here for teenagers. We can ¹*climb* (mcibl) a wooden tower, ² .... (upmj) into the pool and then ³ .... (msiw) to the side. We can ⁴ .... (lyf) a kite or we can ⁵ .... (lisa) in a small boat on the lake. Then, if we're not too tired, we can ⁶ .... (nur) round the lake or ⁷ .... (lypa) tennis with a friend. At the end of the day, there's always a good meal, where we can ⁸ .... (tea) as much as we like!

Prepositions

9 **Look at the picture. Correct the prepositions in the sentences.**

1 There are two people walking ~~down~~ *up* the hill.

2 A man is fishing behind the bridge.

3 Two people are walking under the bridge.

4 There's a wall behind the car park.

5 There's a boy standing on top of the wall.

6 There's a man reading on the trees.

Indefinite pronouns

10 **Complete the conversations with these words.**

~~anyone~~	anything	Everyone	everything
no one	someone	something	

1 **A** Hello! Is there *anyone* at home?
   B There's no noise! Can you hear the TV or
     .... ?
   A No. It looks like there's .... in
     the house.

2 **A** The town is very quiet today!
   B Yes! .... is at home watching
     the football match.
   A Well, I need .... to take me to
     the station!

3 **A** Is .... OK?
   B No, ... is wrong with my leg.

Everyday objects

11 **Match these words to the definitions (1–9).**

camera	jeans	jumper	laptop	magazine
notebook	poster	wallet	~~watch~~	

1 We use this to tell the time.   *watch*
2 This is like a really big photo. We often put it on
  the wall.   ....
3 The name for a small computer you can carry
  in a bag.   ....
4 A book for writing in.   ....
5 We use this to take photos.   ....
6 We keep our money in one of these.
  ....
7 We often read one in the dentist's waiting
  room.   ....
8 This is a pullover.   ....
9 These are a kind of trousers.   ....

School subjects

12 **Match the school subjects (1–8) to the related words (a–h).**

1 Art   **a** kings, queens and wars
2 English   **b** guitars and drums
3 Geography   **c** laboratory, experiments
4 History   **d** algebra, geometry
5 Literature   **e** grammar, vocabulary
6 Maths   **f** Picasso and Van Gogh
7 Music   **g** novels, plays and poems
8 Science   **h** countries, mountains

Present simple: affirmative and negative

13 **Make sentences in the Present simple.**

1 At weekends I / not get up / before ten o'clock
  At weekends, I don't get up before ten o'clock.
2 We / have lunch / at two o'clock
  ....
3 Tina / play / volleyball on Saturdays
  ....
4 Tony never / arrive / on time
  ....
5 Grandad / watch / TV all day
  ....

Present simple: questions and short answers

14 **Complete the questions with these words. Then write the correct verb in the answers.**

Does	drive	~~have~~	like	study

1 Do we *have* any homework for tomorrow? Yes,
  we *do*.
2 .... Lucas work at the weekend?
  No, he ....
3 Do you .... living in the city? Yes,
  I ....
4 Do your parents .... to work? No,
  they ....
5 Does Helen .... history? Yes, she
  ....

Adverbs of frequency

15 **Rewrite the sentences. Put the adverbs of frequency in the correct place.**

1 Sophie remembers phone numbers! (never)
  Sophie never remembers phone numbers!
2 Jo and Ian don't play tennis on Fridays. (usually)
  ....
3 You write to me any more! (hardly ever)
  ....
4 Susan orders chicken at the restaurant. (always)
  ....
5 We don't have time to watch TV! (often)
  ....
6 Ana and her friends go horse-riding. (sometimes)
  ....

Numbers and dates

16 **Write the numbers and dates in words.**

1 60 seconds in a minute *sixty*
2 1 Mar ....
3 5 Jul ....
4 365 days in a year ....
5 1,440 minutes in a day ....
6 100 years in a century ....
7 22 Nov ....

was/were

17 **Choose the correct options.**

A ¹ *Was /* (Were) you at school yesterday?
B Of course I ² *was / were*!
A What about Mary and John? ³ *Was / Were* they at school, too?
B I'm not sure. John ⁴ *was / were* at school all day, but Mary ⁵ *wasn't / weren't* in the Maths class.
A What time ⁶ *was / were* that?
B The Maths class is from 11.30 to 12.30.
A ⁷ *Was / Were* all the other students in Maths?
B Three of the other girls ⁸ *wasn't / weren't* there. They had a special volleyball session yesterday morning.

Opinion adjectives

18 **Complete the adjectives in these sentences.**

1 I hate this song. It's r........................ .
2 That new horror film is really s........................ !
3 This homework is so b........................ .
4 Yes, we've scored! What a b........................ goal!
5 I'm sorry. That joke just isn't f........................ .
6 My mum loves r........................ books.
7 I think mountain biking is the most e........................ sport.
8 My little brother can be very a........................ .
9 This dress is too e........................ . I can't afford it.
10 This meal is really t........................ . Thanks!

Speaking and Listening

1))) 2 **Match the questions (1–6) to the answers (a–f). Then listen and check.**

1 Have you got a favourite school subject? *e*
2 Do you live with your family?
3 What hobbies have you got?
4 Which class were you in last year?
5 What kind of music do you like?
6 Were you at Tina's party last weekend?

a Yes, I was. We had a great time!
b I was in 4D, on the second floor.
c Yes, I do. I live with my mother and my brother.
d I prefer dance music, and I also like soul.
e Yes, I quite like Art.
f Cycling. I go out on my mountain bike every weekend.

2))) 3 **Complete the conversation with these phrases. Then listen and check.**

~~Boring~~	so her classes	To the library
Very funny	What's happening	What subjects

Liam What class have you got next?
Sally Science!
Liam ¹ *Boring*!
Sally No, it isn't! I think Science is quite exciting.
Liam Not for me!
Sally ² .... do you like?
Liam Literature. And our Geography teacher is fun, ³ .... are always interesting.
Sally Right! Where are you going now?
Liam ⁴ .... , to do some research on the internet.
Sally Oh, really? You mean watch videos?
Liam ⁵ .... ! You can't watch videos on the school computers.
Sally Anyway, are you going to Sonia's later?
Liam ⁶ .... at Sonia's?
Sally It's her birthday party!
Liam A party? Brilliant! What time?
Sally Half past seven. But you need to talk to Sonia first!

3 **Read the conversation in Exercise 2 again. Choose the correct options.**

1 Sally (likes) / *doesn't like* Science.
2 Liam likes *two / three* different subjects.
3 Students *can / can't* watch videos in the library.
4 Sonia's party is *today / tomorrow*.
5 Liam *knew / didn't know* about the party.

Home Sweet Home

Vocabulary Rooms and parts of the house

★ **1** Put these words in the correct column.

attic	balcony	cellar	drive
floor	landing	lawn	patio

inside the house	outside the house
attic	

★ **2** Complete the sentences with the words from Exercise 1.

1 Our car's in the garage! You can park in the *drive*.
2 If you want to play ball, go and play on the .... !
3 All my old toys and books are up in the ....
4 We have a big plant on the .... at the top of the stairs.
5 In summer, we often have lunch out on the ....
6 There's a good view of the river from the .... outside my bedroom.
7 Be careful! There's broken glass on the .... in the kitchen!
8 My mum makes jams and marmalades, and keeps them down in the ....

★★ **3** Put the letters in the correct order to complete the text.

It's a wonderful old house. The date above the door says 1820. We had to put on a new ¹ *roof* (foro) last year after the winter storms. The ² .... (ginslice) are high, and some of them are made of wood. There's a ³ .... (freeclapi) in each of the bedrooms, but we don't actually use them. When you go into the house, you go through the ⁴ .... (lalh), and the ⁵ .... (ratsis) are on the left. My mum's ⁶ .... (efocif) is behind them. It's the room with a lot of photos on the ⁷ .... (lawl). Oh, and the ⁸ .... (agrega) has space for two cars. That's on the left side of the building.

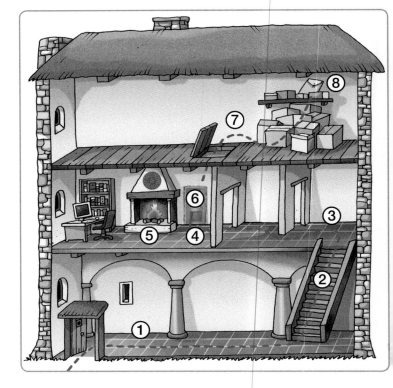

★★ **4** Find the family treasure! Look at the picture. Complete the text with these words.

attic	fireplace	hall	landing
office	roof	stairs	wall

Go through the ¹ *hall* to the ² .... at the end. Then go up to the ³ .... on the first floor. Go along to the left and find the room with the dark red door. This is the ⁴ .... Inside, you can see a desk with a computer, a chair and some books on a shelf. There's also a ⁵ .... in the middle, and in the ⁶ .... next to that, there's a small door. It's not easy to see this door because it looks just like a painting. Open the door and go up into the ⁷ .... Be careful because there's only one small window up there. At one end, there are a lot of old boxes. Under the ⁸ .... above the boxes there's an old brown envelope. Take it down, open it and read what's inside!

Vocabulary page 104

Reading

★ **1** **Read the texts quickly. Choose the best option.**

The texts are …

a a leisure guide to the city.
b adverts from people selling their homes.
c answers to people who want advice.

★ **2** **Complete the sentences.**

1 themansells father has a new *job*.
2 jenwatts has no problems with .... her car.
3 benstarkey has a .... behind the house.
4 stellabailey lives near a football ....
5 jenwatts often travels by ....
6 benstarkey goes shopping by ....

★★ **3** **Complete the sentences with the correct name.**

1 *stellabailey* can see Upton Park from home.
2 .... usually takes the train to the city centre.
3 .... and .... live near some good shops.
4 .... doesn't use transport very much.
5 .... doesn't have any problems with noise.

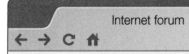

Internet forum

themansells:

We're a family of four and we're looking for a new home in the city. My husband's going to work in a new office, and I'm a hairdresser. We have two young children. Any suggestions for a good area?

jenwatts:

We live in a flat in Midfield, about twenty minutes from the city centre. There are buses every fifteen minutes, so we don't need to use the car every day. Parking isn't a problem because the building has an underground garage. We can hang out the washing on the roof. The shopping's good in this area.

benstarkey:

Our family lives in a house in Felham, about half an hour by train from the city centre. It's a quiet area, without much traffic. We have a small lawn at the front, and a garden at the back with a patio. The children are sitting out there at the moment! I only use the car to go shopping, and I park it in the drive, so it's all quite convenient.

stellabailey:

We live in a rented flat in the city centre, near the stadium. People are coming out of a football match at the moment, so it's a bit noisy, but it's not so bad at night. The shops and restaurants are good, and we can go to most places on foot. Oh, and there's a nice view of Upton Park from our balcony, too!

Grammar Present simple and continuous

★ **1** **Read the text and choose the correct options.**

He [1] *paints / is painting* houses inside and outside. Today he [2] *works / is working* in a flat. First, he [3] *puts / is putting* all the furniture in the middle of the room. Then he [4] *covers / is covering* the furniture with a big cloth before he [5] *starts / is starting* work. At the moment, he [6] *paints / is painting* the edges round the ceiling.

★ **2** **Put the words in the correct order.**

1 Tom / Friday / goes / on / always / a / night / out
Tom always goes out on a Friday night.

2 housework / He / doesn't / with / help / the / usually
....

3 weekend / you / What / do / at / do / normally / the / ?
....
....

4 music / to / Elena's / MP3 / player / her / listening / on
....
....

5 reading / bus / on / isn't / a / magazine / She / the
....
....

6 now / are / What / doing / you / ?
....
....

★★ **3** **Look at the pictures and write sentences.**

1 work / café / serve / coffee
He works in a café, and now he's serving coffee.

2 live / village / visit / city
....

3 sell / fish / talk / phone
....

4 repair / cars / have / break
....

5 drive / taxi / take passenger / station
....

6 go / school / study / Maths
....

★★ **4** **Complete the conversation with the Present simple or Present continuous form of the verbs.**

A Mike, is that you? Are you busy?

M Yes! (I/prepare) [1] *I'm preparing* dinner in the kitchen.

A You in the kitchen? But (you/not normally/cook) [2] ....
.... ! Why (you/cook) [3] ....
today?

M Because my (girlfriend/come) [4] .... for a meal.

A So is it Italian food?

M No, it isn't. (We/only/have) [5] ....
Italian food in restaurants. This is a special Indian meal.

A (you/mean) [6] .... Indian from India?

M Yes, of course!

A But isn't that very spicy food?

M Often yes, but (it/not always/have to) [7] ....
.... be hot!

A OK! Anyway, what's that funny noise I can hear?

M Oh no! The (meat/burn) [8] .... in the pot! That's what happens when I talk too much on the phone!

Vocabulary Furniture and household objects

★★ 5 **Make questions for the underlined answers.**

1 The children are playing in the attic.
Where are the children playing?

2 Right now, we're having a party in the garage!
....
....

3 My sister's studying abroad this year.
....
....

4 Tom's talking to a friend at the moment.
....
....

5 I'm waiting for a bus.
....
....

6 My dad cuts the lawn every two weeks.
....
....

7 We clean the house in the spring.
....
....

8 Yes, we have. We've got a fireplace in the living room.
....
....

9 Kevin usually celebrates his birthday in the cellar!
....
....

★ 1 **Label the numbered objects in the picture.**

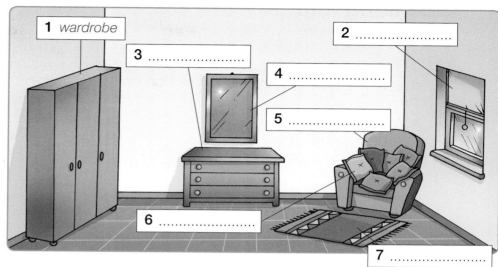

1 *wardrobe*
2 ....
3 ....
4 ....
5 ....
6 ....
7 ....

★ 2 **Complete the sentences with the words from Exercise 1.**

1 The *rug* is on the floor.
2 In front of the left wall, you can see a ....
3 In the corner of the room, there's an .... with .... on it.
4 Above the armchair, you can see a window with a ....
5 On the back wall, there's a .... with a .... above it.

★ 3 **Match these words to the definitions (1–6).**

alarm clock	bookcase	~~curtains~~	duvet	pillow	vase

1 We normally use two of these to cover a window. *curtains*
2 We use this to wake up on time in the morning. ....
3 We use this to keep warm in bed. ....
4 We usually put flowers in one of these. ....
5 We use this in bed for our head. ....
6 We keep books and magazines in this. ....

★★ 4 **Put the letters in the correct order to complete the text.**

This flat's not bad! It's got a big ¹*wardrobe* (rawbored) for my clothes, and there's a ² .... (koboseca) in the living room. I need that for my books because this month I'm doing a course in computing. And there's a desk but no ³ .... (cramhira), but I can bring one from home. What else? There's a ⁴ .... (rorimr) in the bathroom, but I don't see any ⁵ .... (stranuci) on the window, so maybe I can ask my mum to buy some. I don't like all those ⁶ .... (nisshuco) on the sofa – they can go in the cupboard in the bedroom. The bed's OK, but I'll bring my own ⁷ .... (tevud) and a couple of ⁸ .... (lowlips), because I'm more comfortable that way.

Grammar Reference pages 86–87   Vocabulary page 104

Describing a place

Speaking and Listening

★ **1** 〔4〕 **Match the questions (1–6) to the answers (a–f). Then listen and check.**

1 What's your school like? *d*
2 What's your bedroom like?
3 What's that new shopping centre like?
4 What's your holiday apartment like?
5 What's Paula's home town like?
6 What's that new café on Osmond Street like?

a It's very modern. It's got three floors and a café on the roof.
b It's a bit small, but they've got really good music.
c It's quite old, it's on the tenth floor and it's got great views.
d It's really big, with more than a thousand students.
e It's very big and really busy, with lots of shops and traffic.
f It's quite small, but very comfortable, and I've got all my photos on the wall.

★ **2** **Put the conversation in the correct order.**

a And what's your room like? ....
b So where are you living now? .1.
c Are you happy with it then? ....
d It's very noisy and a bit strange. ....
e What's the city like? ....
f Yes, but it's a long way from the centre! ....
g In a rented room in the city. ....
h Well it's really cheap and quite big. ....

★★ **3** 〔5〕 **Complete the conversation with these phrases. Then listen and check.**

| a bit small | a bit strange | ~~Do you mean~~ | quite far |
| really wonderful | that like | the house like | very big |

Olga Hey, Tammi! How are you? I haven't seen you for ages!
Tammi Hi, Olga! I'm just visiting and doing some shopping.
Olga ¹*Do you mean* you don't live here any more?
Tammi Well, we've got a new house on the coast, but I still come to visit my grandparents.
Olga That's very good news! What's ² .... ?
Tammi It's not ³ .... , just two floors, but it's in a lovely area.
Olga I'm sure! And has it got views of the sea?
Tammi Yes, you can see ⁴ .... from the balcony upstairs. And it's got a swimming pool, too, but it's ⁵ ....
Olga And how about the town? What's ⁶ .... ?
Tammi Well, the house is ⁷ .... , because it's five minutes from the beach. But the town is ⁸ .... , and my brothers and I miss our friends.

★ **4** 〔5〕 **Listen to the conversation in Exercise 3 again. Choose the correct options.**

1 Olga and Tammi *know* / *don't know* each other.
2 Tammi *lives* / *doesn't live* with her grandparents.
3 Tammi likes the *location* / *size* of the house.
4 The balcony has *good* / *bad* views.
5 The house is *far from* / *near* the beach.
6 The children are *very happy* / *a bit uncomfortable* in the new town.

★★ **5** **Answer the questions about yourself.**

1 What's your town like? ....
2 What's your school like? ....
3 What's your street like? ....
4 What's your home like? ....
5 What's your room like? ....

Speaking and Listening page 113

Grammar

Verb + -ing

★ 1 **Complete the text with the correct form of these verbs.**

be	get	go	listen
rent	~~see~~	watch	

Living here is very easy. We enjoy ¹ *seeing* the sunshine almost every day, and we love ² .... able to sit outside for meals. We also like ³ .... for long walks in the countryside, which is quite near our flat. And we don't mind ⁴ .... wet when it rains, because it doesn't rain very often. As for going out at night, there are several cinemas, although we sometimes prefer ⁵ .... a DVD to watch at home. There's a theatre too, although we don't go very often. I can't stand ⁶ .... musicals and I don't like ⁷ .... to classical music either!

★ 2 **Put the words in the correct order.**

1 flat / I / stand / ground / living / in / a / on / the / can't / floor
I can't stand living in a flat on the ground floor.

2 with / sleeping / on / She / the / light / prefers

....
....

3 watching / all / Grandma / TV / day / enjoys

....
....

4 housework / with / brother / hates / helping / the / My

....
....

5 out / for / love / a / meal / going / We

....
....

★★ 3 **Write sentences.**

A Do you like living in Athens?
B I / enjoy / live / a big city
¹ *I enjoy living in a big city.*
A And what about the weather?
B I / love / sit / outside in the sun!
² ....
A And the traffic?
B I / not stand / drive / with so many cars / in the streets!
³ ....
A So how do you travel?
B I / like / ride / my bicycle!
⁴ ....
A What about the food?
B I / not mind / try / new foods!
⁵ ....
A And the language?
B I / prefer / speak / English!
⁶ ....
Greek is very difficult for me!

★★ 4 **Write sentences. Use the information in the table.**

	😄 loves	🙂 likes/enjoys	😐 doesn't mind	😟😟 hates/ can't stand
Justin	1 play video games	2 take the dog for a walk	3 wash the car	4 do housework
Leonor	5 get up late at the weekend	6 send texts on her mobile phone	7 help her sister with her homework	8 clean the bath

1 *Justin loves playing video games.*
2 ....
3 ....
4 ....
5 ....
6 ....
7 ....
8 ....

Grammar Reference pages 86– 87

Reading

1 Read the texts quickly. Match the text types (1–3) to the texts (A–C).

1 a postcard
2 a tourist advert
3 an offer of accommodation

A Welcome to Fuengirola in the heart of the Costa del Sol! An ideal holiday destination! In winter, it's a quiet town of 72,000 inhabitants, with very fresh seafood and interesting places to visit. It's ideal for older people. In summer, it's a fantastic place for sun, sand and sea, with a population of 250,000 people! It's very popular with families and young people because there is so much to see and do. With shops, restaurants, clubs, discos – it has nearly everything!

B **HOLIDAY APARTMENT FOR RENT**, in Fuengirola, southern Spain. Large apartment available for July and August. Three double bedrooms, two bathrooms, kitchen and living room. Complete with balcony, underground garage and lift. Fully furnished with beds, wardrobes, a sofa, armchairs and a TV. The kitchen's a bit small but most visitors eat out. For more information, please email fun_fuengirola@costadelsol.com.

C

Dear Mum and Dad,

Here we are at the beach at last! The house we're sharing with friends is small, but we only come back here to shower and change before going out again. Maggie says she hates sitting on the beach all day so she's doing a lot of sports. Tom loves doing nothing so he enjoys lying on the beach and then going out at night. And I prefer doing a little bit of everything so I read, listen to music, go swimming and shopping, and just relax! The weather's a bit hot for me so I don't go to the beach in the middle of the day, but I'm having a wonderful time!

Love,
Linda

Brain Trainer

Underline these words in the texts in Exercise 1:

ideal
for rent
going out

Now do Exercise 2.

2 Complete the sentences.

1 Fuengirola has a lot of *older* visitors in winter.
2 In summer, about 250,000 people .... in Fuengirola.
3 .... people can sleep in the apartment.
4 Parking at the apartment is very ....
5 Linda and her friends don't .... much time in the house.
6 Linda .... go to the beach at midday.

Listening

1 🎧 **6** Listen to the conversation and decide who is talking.

1 a brother and sister
2 two friends
3 two office workers

2 🎧 **6** Listen again. Choose the correct options.

1 The boy prefers the room *with /* *without* the balcony.
2 The girl *likes / doesn't like* the room with the wardrobe.
3 The second room has a *bookcase / desk*.
4 The girl would like to have the *chest of drawers / mirror*.
5 The boy wants a *chest of drawers / desk*.

Writing A description of a room

1 **Rewrite the sentences. Use the linking words.**

  1 I like playing in the attic. I like playing in the cellar. (and)
I like playing in the attic and the cellar.

  2 We enjoy sitting on the balcony. We like sitting on the patio. (also)

....

....

  3 She loves hiding behind the armchairs. She's afraid of going down to the cellar. (but)

....

....

  4 That's his favourite pillow. He doesn't like using a duvet. (however)

....

....

  5 We like having pillow fights. We like playing with cushions. (too)

....

....

  6 I love lying on my grandmother's floor to read. Sheena loves looking at the photos on her walls. (and)

....

....

2 **Look at the picture. Read the text. Correct four mistakes in the text.**

My dream room looks like this. It's quite big and bright, and I can organise it the way I want.

The best things in the room are the bed with its duvet and the rug next to it. Opposite the bed is a bookcase with a TV on one of the shelves. On the wall above the bed there are posters of my favourite musicians and artists. There's a desk in the corner under the window. When I need to study, I just close the blinds. On the wall to the left of the window, there's a board for photos and notes. My papers and school stuff go in the drawers on the right of the desk.

I can lie on the bed listening to music. However, I also need time at my desk. When friends visit, we can play games on the TV, too.

3 **Read the room description again. Put these details in the correct section in column A.**

bright	lie on the bed
papers in the drawers	play video games
~~posters on the wall~~	quite big

	A Picture room	B My dream room
Introduction		*My dream room has …*
Furniture and walls	*posters on the wall*	
Activities		*I can …*

4 **Think of your dream room. Write phrases about it in column B.**

5 **Write a description of your dream room. Use your ideas and information from Exercises 3 and 4.**

Vocabulary Adjectives to describe pictures

★ **1** Put these words in the correct column.

| amusing | blurred | colourful | dramatic | ~~dull~~ | fake |
| horrible | ~~interesting~~ | ~~lovely~~ | old-fashioned | silly | |

one syllable	two syllables	three syllables
dull	lovely	interesting

★ **2** Match the words (1–6) to the definitions (a–f).

1 blurred   f
2 dull
3 fake
4 dramatic
5 old-fashioned
6 silly

a From another period in time, when life was very different.
b It's not serious.
c It's boring, uninteresting.
d It's not real.
e It's exciting, it makes me want to look at it.
f It's not clear; I can't see it very well.

★★ **3** Complete the conversation with these words.

| blurred | dramatic | dull | fake | ~~old-fashioned~~ | silly |

A Look at this! Look at those clothes! And the hairstyles!
B Where did you find that?
A In a box in the attic. The pictures are really ¹ old-fashioned.
B Yeah, I think they must be from the war or something.
A They're a bit ² .... ! There aren't any colours.
B Yes, but sometimes they're very ³ .... Here's one of a building on fire.
A And what's this one?
B I don't know! It's ⁴ .... , so I can't see the detail. It looks like a photo of a person's foot.
A Well, that's a ⁵ .... photo! Why would anyone do that?!
B Who knows! How about this one? It says 'Love from Mount Everest, 1945'.
A That's a ⁶ .... photo! Nobody climbed Mount Everest until 1953!

★★ **4** Put the letters in the correct order to complete the text.

There are many computer programmes for working with photos. Users can create many kinds of ¹ interesting (gritsentien) pictures and effects with the programmes. You can completely change a ² .... (fluoroluc) image by replacing the normal colours with a kind of brown, so you make the image look ³ .... (lod-fadishneo). Or you can change the clothes a person is wearing, and make the picture ⁴ .... (gnusiam). Or again, you can make parts of the image ⁵ .... (delrurb), so that one part becomes more ⁶ .... (cardamit). As people say, the only limit is your imagination! The only problem however, is that it becomes difficult to tell the difference between an original photo and a ⁷ .... (kefa) photo!

Vocabulary page 105

Reading

★ **1** Match the photos (A–C) to the paragraphs (1–3).

★ **2** Complete the sentences.

1 Ulrike *changed* her clothes.
2 In the photo, Danny was
....
3 A storm .... to
the beach last weekend.
4 Danny had his party in a
....
5 A tree .... on to
some cars.
6 Ulrike wasn't ....
to the other people in the
group.

★★ **3** Are the sentences true (T) or false (F)?

1 There were a lot of people at
Danny's party.   *T*
2 Danny's neighbours weren't
happy about the music.   ....
3 Ulrike's group went to the
beach last weekend.   ....
4 Nothing in Ulrike's backpack
was dry.   ....
5 People at the beach were
prepared for the storm.   ....
6 No one was hurt in the
accident.   ....

Brain Trainer

Underline all the
adjectives in
comments 1, 2 and 3.

What do you notice about
a) their form?
b) their position?

Photos

A

B

C

Comments

1

Hi guys! Here's a lovely (but
blurred) picture of Danny's
birthday party! He was
dancing really fast! There
were about forty of us there.
We used his parents' garage
for the party. We stayed late,
but nobody complained
about the music. It was
great!

2

Hey everyone! Here are
some colourful pictures from
our hiking trip last weekend.
My favourite one is of Ulrike
falling into the water. She
was crossing the stream
and listening to music on
her MP3 player. She didn't
hear us warn her about the
moving stones so she fell in.
She didn't hurt herself, but
her backpack got wet, and
everything inside it did, too.
She changed into some dry
clothes that Maria gave to her.

3

How about this for a
dramatic picture? We were
at the beach last weekend
when a sudden storm came.
The winds were really strong
so we left the beach fast.
Then a big palm tree fell on
to some cars parked in the
street. Luckily, there was no
one in the cars. Adrian took
this picture just five minutes
after it happened.

Grammar Past simple

★ **1** Match the questions (1–6) to the answers (a–f).

1 Who took these photos?   *d*
2 Where did she take them?
3 What happened in this one?
4 Did they come out all right?
5 Did Amy upload them to the album?
6 Did anyone else take photos?

a Most of them did, but some are a bit blurred.
b Yes, Jeff took some on his mobile.
c Yes she did – last night.
d Jane did.
e It was at Fran's house on Saturday.
f The flash didn't work!

★★ **2** Complete the text with the correct form of the verbs.

This is a photo of my grandmother, who had an interesting life. When she was fourteen, the war started, and the family [1] *lost* (lose) their business in the city. Her parents [2] .... (not want) to stay in Wales, so they [3] .... (sail) to Argentina. They [4] .... (not speak) Spanish, but there was a Welsh community in Argentina, and her father [5] .... (find) a job there. My grandmother [6] .... (study) in Buenos Aires, where she [7] .... (meet) my grandfather. They got married three years later and had three children, including my father.

★★ **3** Make sentences about Tanya's week. Use the information in the table.

Things to do	Done ✓	Not done ✗
1 tidy my room	✓	
2 wash Dad's car		✗
3 make birthday cake		✗
4 buy new top	✓	
5 reply to emails	✓	
6 check exam marks		✗
7 clean the fireplace	✓	

1 *She tidied her room.*
2 ....
3 ....
4 ....
5 ....
6 ....
7 ....

Past continuous

★ **4** Put the words in the correct order to make answers.

1 A Where were you last weekend?
   B on / I / a / sunbed / lying / was
   I was lying on a sunbed.
2 A What about Saturday night?
   B disco / I / friends / dancing / some / at / was / the / with
   ....
3 A Very interesting! And on Sunday morning?
   B newspapers / We / the / were / morning / reading / all
   ....
4 A And on Sunday afternoon, were you walking in a lovely park?
   B We / park / walking / in / a / on /weren't / Sunday
   ....
5 A So what were you doing on Sunday?
   B We / an / old-fashioned / watching / were / on / film / TV
   ....
6 A What were the people in the film doing?
   B acting / silly / were / They
   ....

★★ **5** Make sentences with the Past continuous form of the verbs.

1 Some children / play / in the garden
   Some children were playing in the garden.
2 A dog / run / in the park
   ....
3 A man / park / his car
   ....
4 A young couple / do / their shopping
   ....
5 Some friends / take / photos
   ....
6 A neighbour / wash / his car
   ....
7 A cat / drink / milk
   ....

Grammar Reference pages 88–89

Vocabulary

Adjective + preposition

★ **1** **Match the sentence beginnings (1–6) to the endings (a–f).**

1 Stella's really good *e*
2 Brian's very interested
3 Old-fashioned pictures are popular
4 Ella's excited
5 We're very proud
6 Jane's keen

a with some collectors.
b on colourful photos.
c in animal photography.
d of our school's prize in the photo competition.
e at taking dramatic photos.
f about seeing her photos in the school magazine.

★ **2** **Choose the correct options.**

1 We don't want to go to the shopping centre because we're *keen on /* *tired of* going there!

2 Don't switch the light off! I'm *afraid of / bad at* the dark.

3 Our team won the game and we were *excited about / angry with* it.

4 She's a very nice person and she's *popular with / proud of* the other students.

5 Our teacher is really *good at / sorry for* telling stories.

6 I want to study music because I am really *bad at / interested in* it.

★★ **3** **Complete the sentences with these words.**

~~afraid~~ angry excited interested keen sorry

1 Everyone said they were *afraid* of traffic accidents.
2 He was .... with them because he didn't get a prize.
3 Several people were very .... on growing their own vegetables.
4 Everyone is .... about the next Olympic Games.
5 She was .... in becoming a writer.
6 Everyone felt .... for the parents with the sick children.

★★ **4** **Complete the text with the correct prepositions.**

This is an interesting picture! You can see this boy on the left: he looks tired ¹ *of* playing with his toys. And the girl on the right, who looks bored ² .... her doll's house. The other children in the middle are laughing and pointing at the screen. It looks like they're quite excited ³ .... a video game. And look at the grandmother's face. She's very proud ⁴ .... her grandchildren! Finally, I feel sorry ⁵ .... the dog next to the boy. It looks afraid ⁶ .... the image of itself in the mirror! This is a lovely picture because it is full of interesting details.

Vocabulary page 105

 **Permission**

Speaking and Listening

★ **1**)) 7 **Put the words in order to make questions. Then listen and check.**

1 Lena / us / you / comes / mind / if / Do / with / ?

Do you mind if Lena comes with us?

2 bicycle / borrow / Can / your / I / ?

....

....

3 if / it / dog / we / OK / take / Is / the / ?

....

....

★ **2**)) 8 **Complete the conversation with the questions from Exercise 1. Then listen and check.**

A Uncle John! a.........................

....

B What do you want it for?

A Kurt and I want to go out for a ride.

B Yes, you can. Just be careful with the traffic.

A b...

....

B Yes, of course! He needs the exercise.

A c *Do you mind if Lena comes with us?*

B Yes, I do! She's got an exam in the morning and she has to study!

★★ **3**)) 9 **Complete the conversation with these words. Then listen and check.**

| Do you mind if | I'm afraid | Is it OK | of course |
| ~~popular with~~ | you can | | |

Guide Good morning and welcome to the Milefoot Country Park! This park is very ¹ *popular with* people who love the countryside. We hope you enjoy your visit.

Man Can we take photos in the park?

Guide Yes, ² .... But we recommend that you don't go too near the animals.

Woman Is it OK if we have a picnic somewhere?

Guide Yes, ³ .... There are special areas with benches where visitors can eat and drink.

Boy ⁴ .... if we go fishing in the river?

Guide No, I'm afraid it isn't. The fish are protected and you can't catch them.

Boy What about a barbecue? ⁵ .... we have a barbecue?

Guide We don't mind if you have picnics, but ⁶ .... you can't have barbecues. It's too dangerous to light fires in the park.

★★ **4**)) 9 **Listen to the conversation in Exercise 3 again. Choose the correct options.**

1 You can / can't see animals in the park.

2 Visitors *should / shouldn't* go near the animals.

3 Visitors can have picnics *anywhere in the park / in special areas*.

4 Fishing *is / isn't* possible.

5 Fires *are / aren't* allowed in the park.

★★ **5** **Write a conversation. Use phrases from Exercises 1–3 above and this information:**

You are staying the weekend at a friend's house. Ask permission to do three different things. Remember to include your friend's replies.

Speaking and Listening page 114

Grammar

Past simple vs Past continuous

★ **1** **Match the sentence beginnings (1–6) to the endings (a–f).**

1 I was having a wonderful dream   *e*
2 A ball hit the woman
3 The girl was texting on her phone
4 The boys saw a bank robbery
5 We were watching a TV report
6 The man fell off his horse

a while he was riding across the river.
b while they were sitting on the balcony.
c while she was walking through the park.
d when we recognised our friends at a concert.
e when the alarm clock woke me up.
f when she put her foot in a hole.

★ **2** **Choose the correct options.**

1 The weather (changed)/ *was changing* while we *came* / (were coming) down the mountain.
2 We *ran / were running* through the woods when Angelica *fell / was falling*.
3 A bird *landed / was landing* on my shoulder while I *ate / was eating* a sandwich!
4 Marla *watched / was watching* TV when her friend *arrived / was arriving*.
5 I *got / was getting* a call while I *waited / was waiting* for the bus.
6 The passengers *sang / were singing* when the plane *took off / was taking off*.

★★ **3** **Make questions for the underlined answers.**

1 I was <u>listening to the radio</u> when I heard the news.
What were you doing when you heard the news?
2 I was listening to the radio when <u>I heard the news</u>.
What happened while you were listening to the radio?
3 Thieves were stealing a painting when <u>the police arrived</u>.
....
4 Thieves were <u>stealing a painting</u> when the police arrived.
....
5 My parents were <u>driving home</u> when the storm started.
....
6 My parents were driving home when <u>the storm started</u>.
....
7 Tania was <u>living abroad</u> when her parents moved house.
....
8 Tania was living abroad when <u>her parents moved house</u>.
....
9 I was <u>filming the concert</u> when the battery died.
....
10 I was filming the concert when <u>the battery died</u>.
....

★★ **4** **Make questions for the missing information.**

1 I was .... when I heard the news.
What were you doing when you heard the news?
2 Our team was .... when the rain started.
....
3 We were .... when the camera battery died.
....
4 Ana was .... when the phone rang.
....
5 My parents were .... when the postman arrived.
....
6 The students were .... when the teacher entered the room.
....

Brain Trainer

Put *when* or *while* into these sentences:

I was having my tea .... the email arrived.
The email arrived .... I was having my tea.

Can you use either word in both sentences?
Look at Grammar Reference page 88 and write the rule.

Grammar Reference pages 88–89

Reading

1 **Read the text quickly. Choose the best title.**

  a An amusing trip to the UK
  b A dramatic trip to the UK
  c A dull trip to the UK

In the spring of 2010, my family was preparing for a trip to the UK. We wanted to go to Scotland to visit Edinburgh, and then to stay in London, to see all the famous places there. We were planning to stay for ten days, and I was really looking forward to the trip.

On 10th April, we flew to Edinburgh and took a taxi to the hotel. The weather was colder than at home, but it was clear and bright. The next three days we went sightseeing. The dungeons on the Royal Mile were really cool! The 14th was our last day there so we went shopping along the famous Princes Street. I got a photo of me with a bagpiper in his kilt, and emailed it to my friends. In the evening, we were having dinner when we saw TV pictures of a volcano erupting in Iceland. The pictures were quite dramatic, but we didn't worry. The next day, we arrived at the airport for the flight to London. But we didn't catch the plane because all the flights were cancelled. Why? Because the ash from the volcano was a serious problem for planes flying over the UK!

In the end, we had to take a train to London, and we spent a whole week sightseeing and shopping in all the famous places. But we had to wait another two days before we could finally catch a flight home. Of course, that was OK with me as I had an extra two days' holiday!

2 **Read the text again. Put these events in the correct order.**

  a go back to Edinburgh airport   ....
  b visit London   ....
  c arrive in Edinburgh   *.1.*
  d see a volcanic eruption on TV   ....
  e visit the dungeons   ....
  f go shopping on Princes Street   ....

Listening

1   ))) 10   **Listen to an interview with a girl who wants to be a photographer. How many photos do they talk about?**

  a 2   **b** 3   **c** 4

2   ))) 10   **Listen again and choose the correct options.**

  1 The photo was of her brother's .... birthday.
    a second
    b third
    c fourth

  2 The bird caught a .... .
    a mouse
    b rabbit
    c cat

  3 She took the photo in Sheffield in .... .
    a spring
    b autumn
    c winter

  4 The colours in the photo were .... .
    a on the buildings
    b on an umbrella
    c in the streets

  5 The two women in the photo were .... .
    a friends
    b sisters
    c mother and daughter

Writing A description of a picture

1 Read the text and correct the sentences.

I took this photo about two years ago, when we were visiting my uncle. He lives abroad, so we don't often see each other. He was living in a new house, and it was the first time that we saw it.

The photo is of a special meal. We cooked paella, which his family had never tried before. The weather was great so we had the meal outside. You can see the lawn and some trees in the background. That's the food on the table in the foreground. That's my uncle and my cousin on the right and my aunt on the left serving the food. Me and my sister are in the middle. We're all laughing because my uncle was telling a joke. I like this photo because it brings back good memories of the time we spent together.

1 This was the family's third visit to the uncle's house.

This was the family's first visit to the uncle's house.

2 They had the meal in the kitchen.

....

3 The food is on the table in the background.

....

4 The people in the photo are crying.

....

5 Her uncle is on the left of the photo.

....

2 Read the text again. Put these phrases in the correct place in column A.

a special meal	good memories
in the background	in the foreground
in the middle	meal outside
new house	on the left
on the right	time together
~~two years ago~~	visit my uncle

	A Picture description	B My photo
Introduction	*two years ago*	
Who/What's the photo and where		
Reasons for choosing the photo		

3 Choose your favourite photo. Write phrases about it in column B.

4 Write a description of your photo. Use your ideas and information from Exercises 2 and 3.

(Introduction)

....
....
....

(Description)

....
....
....
....
....
....

(Conclusion)

....
....
....

Vocabulary Shopping nouns

★ **1** Match (1–6) to (a–f) with make nouns.

1 cash   **a** holder
2 high   **b** basket
3 market   **c** point
4 shop   **d** stall
5 shopping   **e** street
6 stall   **f** assistant

★ **2** Complete the sentences with the nouns from Exercise 1.

1 We often go to the market. One of our friends is a *stallholder* there!
2 When you enter our supermarket, please take a ....
3 The best shops here are in the ....
4 Do you need money? The nearest .... is opposite the bus station.
5 Let's meet at the .... where they sell sweets.
6 We asked the .... where to find the sports department.

★ **3** Match these words to the definitions (1–6).

bargain	change	customer
products	queue	sale

1 This is a special time when shop prices are cheaper. *sale*
2 This is the name for the things we buy in shops. ....
3 This is the money you get back if you pay too much. ....
4 This is when you buy something good at a very low price. ....
5 This is the name for the person who wants to buy something. ....
6 This is where you have to wait when there are a lot of people who want to do the same thing.
....

Vocabulary page 106

★★ **4** Complete the text with these words.

cashpoint	change	coin	market stall
notes	price	queue	stallholder

At about 11 o'clock, he stopped at a ¹*cashpoint* to get some money. He had to wait in the ² .... for a while. Then he put the ³ .... in his wallet. Next, he went to a ⁴ .... where they were selling shoes. But he didn't buy any. The ⁵ .... didn't look very happy. Maybe there was a problem with the ⁶ .... A small boy near the stall was asking for money. I saw the man give the boy a ⁷ .... Then he went to a café, where he talked on his mobile phone. When he finished his coffee, he paid the waiter and left the ⁸ .... on the table.

Reading

Markets or supermarkets?

At *Shopping Trends* magazine, we asked for our readers' opinions, and here is what they said.

Well I live in a quiet village without many shops, and no market. The nearest market is in the big town half an hour away, and there aren't enough buses to get there. So for me, supermarkets are the best option. I can simply park the car and do the shopping. It's more convenient and there's a bigger variety of products than at a market. And markets, for me personally, aren't clean enough.

Sandra

There's a good market near my flat, so it's easier for me to do my shopping there. Their prices are about the same as at the supermarket but they give a better service. I only go to the supermarket when the market is closed.

Trish

I'm a real fan of markets – indoor markets or street markets. They're much noisier than supermarkets, but that's all part of the fun! I think the products are fresher, too. Supermarket fruit, for example, looks good but doesn't taste good enough for me. Markets are usually a bit cheaper too, and always friendlier. The stallholders know me so they know what I want.

Matt

★ **1** **Write the correct names.**

1 .... clearly prefers markets.

2 .... clearly prefers supermarkets.

3 .... prefers markets but shops at both.

★ **2** **Complete the sentences.**

1 There isn't a *market* where Sandra lives.

2 Trish likes the .... she gets at the market.

3 Matt prefers the .... food they sell in markets.

4 Trish goes to the supermarket when the market is ....

5 Matt likes markets because they are .... and friendlier.

★★ **3** **Choose the correct option.**

1 (Sandra) / Matt thinks markets are a bit dirty.

2 *Trish / Matt* prefers the fruit from markets.

3 *Sandra / Trish* thinks that prices are very similar.

4 *Trish / Matt* knows that supermarkets are quieter places to shop in.

5 *Sandra / Matt* doesn't have a market near her/his home.

6 *Sandra / Trish* can't always get to the market when it's open.

Grammar Comparatives and superlatives

★ **1** Put the words in the correct order.

1 sister's / is / mine / comfortable / My / than / room / more

My sister's room is more comfortable than mine.

2 town / are / the / beach / The / nearer / our / mountains / than

....

....

3 shop / in / is / the / town / Benson's / cheapest

....

4 market stall / best / has / This / the / products

....

....

5 world / popular / the / The / most / internet / market / the / is / in

....

....

6 bargains / supermarket / The / has / than / our / shops / better / local

....

....

★★ **2** Complete the text with the correct form of the adjectives.

My parents say it's important to save money when we buy things. Clothes and shoes are often ¹ *cheaper* (cheap) in the street market, but normal shops usually have ² .... (good) quality. The local department store always has the ³ .... (good) selection, but it's also the ⁴ .... (expensive) shop in town! However, they have the ⁵ .... (popular) sales too, because you can find really good bargains there. My friends say it's ⁶ .... (easy) to do all the shopping in one big store, but I say it's ⁷ .... (interesting) to visit different places and compare prices and quality.

★★ **3** Write sentences. Use the information in the table.

	Todds	Ekomart	Breezer
Distance from town centre	0.5 km	1.5 km	4 km
Service (good)	★★	★★★	★
Assistants (friendly)	★	★★	★★★
Prices (expensive)	★★★	★★	★

(★ = minimum)

1 Ekomart / Todds / distance
Ekomart is further from the town centre than Todds.

2 Ekomart / Todds / service

....

3 Breezer / Todds / service

....

4 Ekomart / Todds / assistants

....

5 Ekomart / Breezer / prices

....

6 Breezer / distance
Breezer is the furthest from the town centre.

7 Ekomart / service

....

8 Breezer / service

....

9 Breezer / assistants

....

too and enough

★ **4** Complete the conversation with *too* or *enough*.

A Do you want to go swimming?

B Not really! It's ¹ *too* cold today. What about the cinema?

A No, I haven't got ² .... money for that!

B Let's go out on the bikes then!

A I'm ³ .... tired! I played football all afternoon yesterday. What did you do?

B My homework! I didn't have ⁴ .... time to do anything else.

A OK! Was that your Maths homework?

B Yes, it was.

A Great! So you can help me with mine! I tried, but it was ⁵ .... difficult.

B I'm not sure about that. Your problem is that you don't have ⁶ .... patience!

Vocabulary Money verbs

★★ **5** Kelly doesn't really want to go to Dylan's party. Write sentences, using *too* or *enough*.

Kelly doesn't really want to go to Dylan's party.

Sorry Dylan, but …

1 party / finish / late.
the party finishes too late.

2 I / busy / at home

....
....

3 I / not have got / time

....
....

4 your flat / far / my house

....
....

5 bus / not stop / near

....
....

6 I / not have got / money / buy / a present

....
....

7 party dress / not new

....
....

8 I / tired

....
....

★ **1** Match the sentence beginnings (1–6) to the endings (a–f).

1 Good morning! I'd like to borrow
2 How would you like to pay
3 I'm afraid you don't earn
4 Excuse me! Do these cost
5 Teri's family are going to sell
6 For petrol, I always pay

a €6.50 or €8.50?
b by credit card.
c their house.
d for your new suit?
e some money for a Porsche.
f enough for a car like that.

★ **2** Complete the adverts with these verbs.

afford	lend	pay in cash	~~Buy~~	Save	Win

① *Buy* **2, get 1 free!**

② .... **HUNDREDS of prizes in our new competition!**

③ .... £50 *with our special offers!*

④ **Best prices in town for your old mobile phones! We .... !**

⑤ **Do you need money urgently? We .... instant cash! ASK INSIDE.**

⑥ **WINTER SALES – AT PRICES YOU CAN** .... **!**

★★ **3** Choose the correct options.

1 Did you know? Your brother (won) / earned a new bicycle in a competition!
2 Tamara needed money for the trip, so I *borrowed / lent* her €50.
3 She *bought / cost* her mother a new watch for her birthday.
4 Ellen *paid / sold* her old laptop for £40.
5 It wasn't very expensive, so we *afforded / paid in cash*.
6 The concert was fantastic! I *earned / spent* £80 on T-shirts for my friends.

★★ **4** Complete the text with these verbs.

afford	borrowed	~~cost~~	earned	paid by credit card	saved

Paula wanted a new smart phone, but it ¹*cost* €400, and she couldn't ² .... it. She ³ .... the money from her birthday presents, she ⁴ .... some extra money by doing some work for the neighbours, and she ⁵ .... the last €50 from her mother. Finally, she and her mother went to the shop and her mother ⁶ .... Paula's mother says it's better to do that because sometimes there are problems with the products you buy.

Grammar Reference pages 90–91

Vocabulary page 106

 **Asking for help**

Speaking and Listening

★ **1** 🔊 11 **Match the questions (1–6) to the answers (a–f). Then listen and check.**

1 Could you give me change for the coffee machine ?   *c*
2 Would you mind taking a photo for us?
3 Can you pass me the sugar?
4 Could you give me a hand with these boxes?
5 Would you mind driving me to the station?
6 Could you post this letter for me?

a Sorry, I can't. I don't drive.
b Sure. Do you want a spoon, too?
c Sorry, I can't. I've only got notes.
d OK. There's a post office next to my school.
e No problem. Where are you going to stand?
f Sorry, I can't. I've got a pain in my back.

★ **2** 🔊 12 **Put the conversation in the correct order. Then listen and check.**

a Good idea! Can you get them? They're too high for me.
b I think so. Would you mind paying for this?   ....
c How about some of those snacks?   ....
d Sorry, I can't. I haven't got any cash.   ....
e What else do we need for the party?   .1.
f Sure. Is that everything?   ....

★ **3** 🔊 13 **Complete the conversation with these words. Then listen and check.**

~~Can~~   Could   give   mind   problem   Sorry

Lucy	Pippa!
Pippa	What?
Lucy	¹*Can* you help me to choose a camera? I don't know which one to buy.
Pippa	OK. What kind do you prefer?
Lucy	I want one I can use in the swimming pool.
Pippa	I don't know about those! Let's ask the shop assistant. Excuse me! ²........................ you show us some cameras for taking pictures under water?
Shop assistant	No ³........................ ! This one is very popular.
Lucy	Would you ⁴........................ taking a photo for us?
Shop assistant	⁵........................ , I can't. You have to buy the camera first!
Lucy	What do you think, Pippa?
Pippa	It's your money!
Lucy	OK, I'll buy it. Can you ⁶........................ me a hand with these bags? I need to find my money.
Pippa	Sure!

★★ **4** 🔊 13 **Listen to the conversation in Exercise 3 again. Complete the sentences with one word.**

1 Lucy wants to *buy* a new camera.
2 She asks Pippa to .... her choose one.
3 They decide to ask the shop ....
4 They also ask him to .... a photo for them.
5 But the shop assistant says that's not ....
6 In the end, Lucy .... to buy the camera.

★★ **5** **Write a conversation. Use phrases from Exercises 1–3 and this information:**

You are shopping for clothes with a friend. Ask them to help you decide on three different items. Remember to include their replies.

Speaking and Listening page 115

Grammar *much, many, a lot of*

★ **1** Match the pictures (A–F) to the sentences (1–6).

1 He's got a lot of pets.   *E*
2 She's got too much furniture.
3 She hasn't got much furniture.
4 He's got too many pets.
5 He hasn't got many pets.
6 She's got a lot of furniture.

★ **2** Choose the correct options.

1 How *much /* (*many*) cinemas are there in your town?
2 There are a *lot of / much* people waiting in the queue.
3 There aren't *much / many* good films to watch this week.
4 We don't have *much / many* time before the film starts.
5 How *much / many* money do we need?
6 Don't take *a lot of / too many* food with you!

★★ **3** Write sentences with *too much* and *too many*.

1 She / have got / old toys / her room.
   She's got too many old toys in her room.
2 Our parents think / my sister / spend / time / on the phone
   ....
   ....
3 My mother says / I / spend / money / on shoes
   ....
   ....
4 I think my friends / spend / time / on the internet
   ....
   ....
5 My brother says / I have / hobbies
   ....
   ....
6 There / be / salt / in the soup!
   ....
   ....

★★ **4** Complete the conversation with these words and phrases.

How many	~~How much~~	many	much
too many	too much		

A Those shoes are nice! ¹*How much* did they cost?
B They were €49.50 in the sales!
A You were lucky! I didn't see ² .... shoes I liked.
B What about your top? Is that new as well?
A Yes! Do you like it? It didn't cost ³ .... ! Only about €10.
B Really? ⁴ .... did you buy?
A I bought four!
B Wow! I wanted to buy more shoes, but my mum says I've got ⁵ .... shoes already.
A Yes! My mum says I spend ⁶ .... money on clothes, too. But if it's birthday money, I can spend it on what I like.

Grammar Reference pages 90–91

Reading

1 Read the text quickly. Match the headings (1–3) to the paragraphs (A–C).

1 How do we recognise a shopaholic?
2 What can we do about it?
3 What exactly is the problem?

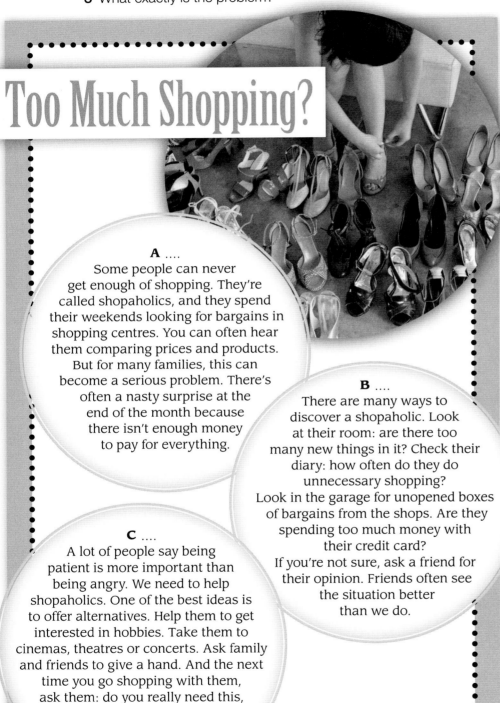

Too Much Shopping?

A ....
Some people can never get enough of shopping. They're called shopaholics, and they spend their weekends looking for bargains in shopping centres. You can often hear them comparing prices and products. But for many families, this can become a serious problem. There's often a nasty surprise at the end of the month because there isn't enough money to pay for everything.

B ....
There are many ways to discover a shopaholic. Look at their room: are there too many new things in it? Check their diary: how often do they do unnecessary shopping? Look in the garage for unopened boxes of bargains from the shops. Are they spending too much money with their credit card? If you're not sure, ask a friend for their opinion. Friends often see the situation better than we do.

C ....
A lot of people say being patient is more important than being angry. We need to help shopaholics. One of the best ideas is to offer alternatives. Help them to get interested in hobbies. Take them to cinemas, theatres or concerts. Ask family and friends to give a hand. And the next time you go shopping with them, ask them: do you really need this, or is it better for you to save the money for something more important?

2 Are the sentences true (T) or false (F)?

1 A shopaholic is a person who spends too much time shopping. *T*
2 Shopaholics don't usually spend much money. ....
3 A person with many new things they don't need may be a shopaholic. ....
4 Inviting a shopaholic to a dance class would be a good idea. ....
5 It's a good idea to be angry with shopaholics. ....
6 We don't need to think much before we go shopping. ....

Listening

1))) 14 Listen to four radio adverts. Number the adverts in the order you hear them.

a a chance to win a prize ....
b free entry to a disco ....
c special offer furniture *.1..*
d tickets by phone ....

2))) 14 Listen again and complete the details.

1 The furniture shop closes at *8 p.m.*
2 The date for Mike Springston's concert is ....
3 The bicycle shop opens at ....
4 Only .... customers can have free entry to the disco.

Brain Trainer

Look at Grammar Reference page 90 and then put *much* and *many* into this sentence.

Too .... people have too .... money.

Now write the rule.

Writing A customer review

1 Read the review. Match the headings (A–D) to the paragraphs (1–4).

    A What I didn't like about the restaurant   *3*
    B My general opinion about the restaurant
    C What I liked about the restaurant
    D General information about the restaurant

Spanish restaurants

Pepe's Taberna

'Lighting poor, restaurant noisy'

★★★☆☆   Reviewed 30 June 2013

① Pepe's Taberna is a Spanish restaurant in the town centre. It's only five minutes from a bus stop, and it opens six days a week (they close on Mondays), from 12.00 midday until midnight. There are tables for a maximum of 80 people.

② We went there for lunch. We ordered a big salad and paella, their special rice dish. There was a good selection of soft drinks. The salad was very fresh, and the rice was tasty. The waiters were friendly and attentive, and the prices are very reasonable.

③ However, I don't think the lighting is very good. It's too dark to see what you're eating. I also found it difficult to chat to my friends because it's a bit noisy: the tables are very close together and you can hear other people's conversations.

④ In my opinion, it's a good place for a quick lunch when you're shopping. But it's not the best place for a romantic dinner!

Visited June 2013

Was this review helpful?   **Yes**

2 Read the review again. Add these words to the correct section in column A.

attentive	fresh
friendly	good selection
~~midday till midnight~~	noisy
reasonable	six days a week
~~Spanish food~~	tasty
too dark	~~town centre~~
good place for a quick lunch	
not for a romantic dinner	

	A Pepe's Taberna	B My restaurant/ café: ....

1 location
   kind of food/ cooking
   opening times
	town centre
	Spanish food
	midday till midnight	

2 food and drink
   prices
   service		

3 atmosphere		
4 recommendation		

3 Now think of a restaurant or café you visited recently. Write the name at the top of column B. Then write information and ideas in column B.

4 Write a review. Use your ideas and information from Exercises 2 and 3.

1 ....
....
....

2 ....
....
....

3 ....
....
....

4 ....
....
....

Check Your Progress 1

Grammar

1 **Complete the conversation with the Present simple or Present continuous form of the verbs.**

A Hi, Tom! [0]*Are* (be) you busy?

B Not really. I [1]....................... (check) my emails, that's all.

A Anything interesting?

B One of my friends [2]....................... (want) me to help him paint his room.

A Where [3]....................... (he/live)?

B It's about twenty minutes by bus. But he's got a swimming pool!

A That sounds OK, if you [4]....................... (not mind) the work.

B So what [5]....................... (you/do) now?

A I [6]....................... (wait) for Angela. I have to talk to her.

/ 6 marks

2 **Complete the text with the Past simple or Past continuous form of the verbs.**

Hi Mandy!

How are you? [0]*Did you have* (you/have) a good weekend? I have to tell you the story of what [1]....................... (happen) yesterday! Kev and I were in that new shopping centre near the park. We [2]....................... (look) for some shoes in the sales, when we [3]....................... (see) some really nice ones in a shop window. The shop assistant [4]....................... (bring) them out and Kev [5]....................... (try) them on when this boy [6]....................... (take) Kev's old shoes and ran away! Amazing! Kev had to buy the new shoes anyway and I [7]....................... (feel) sorry for him because they weren't very cheap.

Write soon,
Amy

/ 7 marks

3 **Choose the correct options.**

0 Tom loves .... cards, but I prefer video games!
   a play   **b** playing   **c** when play

1 Ana always gets better marks .... Albert.
   a that   **b** than   **c** to

2 Their car is old-fashioned; our car is much .... !
   a most modern
   b more modern
   c least modern

3 He's .... boy in the world.
   a the happier   **b** happiest   **c** the happiest

4 Rita bought .... jacket in the shop!
   a the most expensive
   b too expensive
   c the more expensive

5 Marta is .... excited about the trip. She can't sleep!
   a enough   **b** too   **c** much

6 I'd love to buy the coat, but I don't have .... money!
   a many   **b** too   **c** enough

7 Tammi doesn't mind waiting! She's got .... time.
   a a lot of   **b** much   **c** many

/ 7 marks

Vocabulary

4 **Choose the correct options.**

0 Excuse me! How much does this .... ?
   a buy   **b** price   **c** cost

1 You can leave your bags on the .... at the top of the stairs
   a lawn   **b** patio   **c** landing

2 Reception? There's no .... on my bed!
   a blind   **b** pillow   **c** rug

3 My parents keep a lot of old stuff down in the .... .
   a ceiling   **b** cellar   **c** roof

4 Paul isn't very .... insects, but I think they're very interesting!
   a keen on   **b** good at   **c** tired of

5 I can't see this photo very well – it's too .... .
   a colourful   **b** dramatic   **c** blurred

6 The difference between the two parts of the photo is unreal. I think it's .... .
   a dull   **b** fake   **c** horrible

7 Jake doesn't have many friends. I feel .... him.
  a proud of
  b excited about
  c sorry for

8 Excuse me! The .... to pay for things is over there!
  a queue
  b cashpoint
  c customer

9 There's a street market in town today! Let's see if we can find a .... .
  a coin
  b bargain
  c shop assistant

10 I'd love to buy these shoes, but I can't .... them.
  a cost   **b** save   **c** afford

/ 10 marks

Speaking

5 **Complete the conversations with these words and phrases.**

a bit	Can you	give me a hand
like	No problem	Would you mind

A Can I ask you something?
B ⁰ *No problem.*
A Could you ¹....................... with these boxes?
B OK! Where do you want them?
A I need to take them up to the attic.
B An attic? There's no attic in my flat! What's it ²....................... ?
A Nothing special! There aren't any windows, so it's ³....................... dark. ⁴....................... opening the door first?
B No problem. Is it up these stairs?
A That's right.
B ⁵....................... go first then? I don't know the way.
A Sure!

Can	I don't	I'm afraid it isn't	Is it OK	mind if

A Dad! ⁶....................... if we play football in the garden?
B Six boys together? No, ⁷....................... . The garden isn't big enough!
A ⁸....................... we play music in the garage then?
B Yes, that's all right, but I'll take the car out first.
A Do you ⁹....................... we get pizzas for supper?
B No, ¹⁰....................... . But you must clean the kitchen when you finish!

/ 10 marks

Translation

6 **Translate the sentences.**

1 I don't have enough money to buy the CD.
....

2 Could you tell me where the nearest cashpoint is?
....

3 That shop sells the tastiest sandwiches in town!
....

4 Can I borrow €20 to go to the street market?
....

5 I was going home on the bus when she called me.
....

/ 5 marks

Dictation

7))) 15   **Listen and write.**

1 ....
2 ....
3 ....
4 ....
5 ....

/ 5 marks

4 In The News

Vocabulary News and media

★ **1** Label the pictures with these words and *news*.

flash	international	~~local~~	national
paper	presenter	website	

1 *local news*
2 ....
3 ....
4 ....
5 ....
6 ....
7 ....

★ **2** Match these words to the definitions (1–7).

blog	current affairs programme	headline
~~interview~~	journalist podcast	report

1 When one person asks someone else a lot of official questions.   *interview*
2 Personal news and comments from an individual on a webpage.   ....
3 This is the person who finds and presents information for a newspaper.   ....
4 This is the name for the information which they present.   ....
5 This is the title for a newspaper story.

....
6 News in the form of audio files for downloading from the internet.   ....
7 Where people present and comment on events in the news.   ....

★ **3** Match the sentence beginnings (1–8) to the endings (a–h).

1 My sister loves clothes   *e*
2 I don't know all the details
3 We heard about a tsunami
4 She often uses her smartphone
5 My father always reads news stories
6 Opinion articles are not the same
7 I love our local newspaper
8 Sean has no time to read newspapers

a but he often listens to podcasts.
b written by the same journalist.
c to access a news website.
d because I recognise people and places in it.
e and reads a fashion blog every week.
f on a newsflash this morning.
g because I only read the headlines.
h as serious news reports.

★★ **4** Put the letters in the correct order to complete the text.

I don't mind watching the news on TV, like my parents, but I'm not interested in those
[1] *current affairs* (truncer frasifa) programmes, where the news [2] .... (erserpent) introduces a topic and then
[3] .... (winevestir) people who know more about it. And then they all give their opinions. I only look at the newspaper for the football, but my uncle's a
[4] .... (jolisaturn), and he says I should read the [5] .... (delihsane), and then the full [6] .... (perrot) if I want to. But it's easier for me to access a news
[7] .... (ebistew): they've got the news in pictures, on video and in audio files, too. And the best part is the [8] .... (globs), because you can always find one on a topic you like.

Vocabulary page 107

Reading

Brain Trainer

Underline these words in the text in Exercise 1:

the news
blog
social networks
newspapers

Now do Exercise 1.

★ **1** Read the texts quickly and match the people (1–3) to their news priorities (a–c).

1 Esther
2 her brother
3 her parents

a current affairs
b pop culture
c sports

★ **2** Match the phrases (1–6) with the gaps (a–f) in the text.

1 on his mobile phone as well
2 blogs if they have them
3 you can't even talk to them
4 just a few things
5 that's boring for us
6 Billy reads that regularly, too

★★ **3** Are the sentences true (T) or false (F) ?

1 Esther prefers cartoons to news. *T*
2 Her parents are only interested in the news at weekends. ....
3 Her brother buys a special sports magazine. ....
4 Billy follows his friend's news from New Delhi. ....
5 Esther enjoys reading a friend's blog. ....

interview with ESTHER

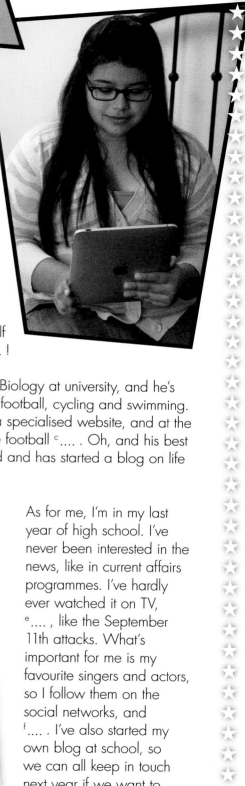

We asked Esther to tell us how her family get their news. This is what she said.

My mum and dad are still kind of traditional. They've always watched the news on TV at lunchtime. I mean, ª .5. , because we can't watch the cartoons on the other channel. Plus at the weekends, they've always bought the Sunday newspapers. Then they spend half the morning reading them, so ᵇ.... !

My elder brother Billy is studying Biology at university, and he's always been keen on sports, like football, cycling and swimming. He gets all his sports news from a specialised website, and at the weekends he gets updates on the football ᶜ.... . Oh, and his best friend from school is living abroad and has started a blog on life in New Delhi. So ᵈ.... .

As for me, I'm in my last year of high school. I've never been interested in the news, like in current affairs programmes. I've hardly ever watched it on TV, ᵉ.... , like the September 11th attacks. What's important for me is my favourite singers and actors, so I follow them on the social networks, and ᶠ.... . I've also started my own blog at school, so we can all keep in touch next year if we want to.

Grammar Present perfect

★ **1** Match the sentence beginnings (1–6) to the endings (a–f).

1 I've been to France
2 She's had that toy
3 We've had
4 Have you ever
5 What have you
6 Where have you

a put your dad's newspaper?
b done with your gym bag?
c had a bad dream?
d some very bad weather recently.
e since she was five.
f but I've never been to Austria.

★ **2** Complete the first lines of newspaper reports with the correct form of these verbs.

appear	arrive	discover	~~escape~~
interview	open	present	record

1 **A grey-haired monkey has** *escaped* **from the zoo.**

2 **A local schoolgirl has** .... **a podcast at the radio station.**

3 **The mayor has** .... **the new theme park in the city.**

4 **The high school drama club has** .... **on the national news.**

5 **An American journalist has** .... **an award to the city.**

6 **Local History teachers have** .... **a Viking ship in the river.**

7 **A local schoolboy has** .... **Adele about her new album.**

8 **25 Swedish schoolchildren have** .... **in town on an exchange visit.**

★ **3** Complete the questions with the Present perfect form of these verbs. Then add the correct verb in the answers.

1 *Have you ever climbed* (you/ever climb) a volcano? No, I *haven't*.

2 .... (your brother/ever do) the housework? No, he ....

3 .... (your parents/ever travel) to the USA? No, they ....

4 .... (your family/ever visit) Paris? Yes, they ....

5 .... (you/ever buy) an expensive present? Yes, I ....

6 .... (your friend/ever lose) a mobile phone? Yes she ....

★ **4** Put the words in the correct order.

1 America / wanted / Maite / has / to / visit / always
Maite has always wanted to visit America.

2 written / you / English / ever / someone / to / Have / in / ?
....
....

3 interested / comics / always / in / has / Paul / manga / been
....
....

4 the / have / camping / weekend / gone / often / at / We
....
....

5 tried / a / Have / face / draw / you / person's / ever / to / ?
....
....

6 gone / parents / without / Have / holiday / your / ever / on / you / ?
....
....

7 been / on / your / ever / family / Has / TV / ?
....
....

8 competition / Has / a / team / ever / your / football / won / national / ?
....
....

Vocabulary Adverbs of manner

★★ 5 **Complete the conversation with the correct form of the verbs.**

A Why don't you write a report for our school blog?

B Me? I ¹ *'ve never written* (never/write) a report in my life!

A Not even in the English class?

B I don't think so!

A ² .... (you/ever interview) someone?

B No. I'm not a news presenter! Have you?

A Yes, I ³ .... (interview) three or four people.

B And how many reports ⁴ .... (you/do)?

A Three.

B Well, you would have to help me, then. ⁵ .... (you/think) about a person to interview?

A The school bus driver must have some interesting stories!

B OK. I'll think of the questions. Can you show me how to organise the report?

A Sure! I ⁶ .... (prepare) that for you already. Here you are!

★ 1 **Match the questions (1–6) to the answers (a–f).**

1 Does Carlos write well? *d*
2 How fast can you run?
3 Do your friends work hard?
4 How well can you speak German?
5 Could you speak more slowly, please?
6 How early do you want to leave?

a Sorry, I didn't realise I was speaking so fast.
b Yes, they do. Very hard!
c About 7.00 a.m., so we don't arrive late!
d I think he writes very clearly.
e I can do a kilometre in ten minutes!
f Not so well, but I'm getting better all the time.

★ 2 **Complete the sentences with the opposite adverb.**

1 Jim plays the guitar well, but he sings *badly*.
2 She always drives carefully, but last night she drove ....
3 The children played happily on the floor, but their mother looked .... at the news flash.
4 Magda reads fast in her own language, but she reads .... in English.
5 I like to get home early – but sometimes the bus is .... !
6 Mum! Don't speak so loudly on the phone! We're trying to work .... in our room.

★ 3 **Choose the correct options.**

A So, Alan. What's it like to be a blog writer?

B It's a lot of fun! I can be sitting ¹ *carelessly /* (*quietly*) at the computer when my mobile phone rings ² *slowly / loudly* and it's a friend with a good idea for a story. So I check the details ³ *early / carefully*, and then upload my comments. I don't like to work too ⁴ *fast / angrily*, because that's when I make mistakes.

A So do a lot of people write back?

B It depends, really. Sometimes I can wait ⁵ *patiently / sadly* at the computer and nothing happens. Other times people will ⁶ *happily / late* upload a dozen comments in ten minutes!

★★ 4 **Complete the text with the adverb form of the words.**

I was waiting ¹ *patiently* (patient) for a bus the other day, when a dog appeared and started barking ² .... (loud). I'm usually a bit scared of dogs, and there was no one else around. I thought ³ .... (hard) for a moment, and then remembered I had a biscuit in my pocket. So I took it out ⁴ .... (careful) and gave it to the animal. It stopped barking at once and wagged its tail ⁵ .... (happy). So then I touched it and talked to it, and ⁶ .... (slow) we became friends. The dog's been at home now for three weeks!

Grammar Reference pages 92–93

Vocabulary page 107

Speaking and Listening

★ **1** ◖🔊 16◗ **Choose the correct options. Then listen and check.**

1 A I've just seen Matt Damon at the airport!
  B *Come on then! / You're joking!*
  A Oh yes? Switch on the TV!

2 A Have you heard the news?
  B What?
  A Scotland have won the European Cup!
  B *That's impossible! / Go ahead!* They didn't even qualify!

3 A Hey! Our History teacher has written a book!
  B *I don't mind. / I don't believe it!*
  A She has! There's a copy in the library.

4 A Hi guys! Have you seen this?
  B What is it?
  A An autograph from Rihanna.
  B *No problem! / No, really?*
  A It is! My cousin works at the stadium.

5 A Brilliant! We've got a holiday tomorrow!
  B *That's strange! / That's a shame!* Tomorrow's Wednesday. Why don't you check the calendar?

6 A Have you read the paper?
  B What's happened?
  A They're closing the local gym!
  B *I'd like that! / That's ridiculous!* They only opened it last year!

★ **2** ◖🔊 17◗ **Put the sentences in the correct order. Then listen and check.**

a What news?   ....
b No, I'm not! Look, here's a photo!   ....
c Why not?   ....
d Have you heard the news?   *1.*
e Yes, but it says they can't sell them.   ....
f Because they don't have enough factories
  to build them!   ....
g You're joking!   ....
h They've invented a car that runs on
  hydrogen!   ....

★ **3** ◖🔊 18◗ **Complete the conversation with these phrases. Then listen and check.**

| Are you sure | I don't believe it | ~~something scary~~ |
| strange lights | that's not all | the best part |

A Have you seen this story about a camel?
B No! What happened?
A This tourist was driving along when he saw
  ¹*something scary* on the road ahead, and
  made an emergency stop.
B So? That sounds normal!
A In the desert, in the middle of the night?
  There were ²....................... moving as well!
B No, really?
A Yes, but ³....................... ! He thought it was
  an alien from space!
B You're joking!
A No – that's what it says here. So he called the
  police.
B ⁴....................... !
A Yes, but ⁵....................... is still to come!
B What's that?
A They told him that police put light strips on
  many camels in order to prevent traffic
  accidents!
B Amazing! ⁶....................... that's a real story?!

★★ **4** ◖🔊 18◗ **Listen to the conversation in Exercise 3 again. Are the sentences true (T) or false (F).**

1 The driver was a local man.   *F*
2 The story took place in a desert.   ....
3 He was very confused about what he saw.   ....
4 He phoned his wife.   ....
5 The police explained the strange
  phenomenon.   ....

★★ **5** **Write a conversation. Use expressions from Exercises 1–3 and this information:**

You tell a friend an amazing story you heard on TV. Your friend isn't sure if the story is real. Remember to include your friend's responses.

Speaking and Listening page 116

Grammar Present perfect vs Past simple

★ **1** Match the beginnings of the news reports (1–6) to the endings (a–f).

1 A cat has attacked a large dog.   *d*
2 A local family has reported seeing UFOs near the river.
3 The high school's website has reached 5,000 visits.
4 A local girl has won a national blog-writing competition.
5 High school students have recorded a podcast for the town council.
6 The local newspaper has introduced a news section for teenagers.

a The school's principal said last year's maximum was only 2,400 visits.
b The paper said the section was requested by teens.
c They made the recording in English for tourists.
d When the cat found itself in a corner, it jumped on the dog.
e Elena Márquez got first prize for her fashion blog last weekend.
f Both parents and children said they saw strange shapes in the sky.

Family sees UFOs.

★ **2** Choose the correct options.

1 Steve *has broken / broke* his arm last weekend.
2 My bicycle *has disappeared / disappeared*.
3 Firemen *have rescued / rescued* three people from a lift yesterday.
4 My grandmother *has had / had* an operation!
5 A teenager *has won / won* this year's national chess contest.
6 Five thousand people *have attended / attended* the local music festival.
7 We *have lost / lost* our suitcases!
8 A young woman *has had / had* a baby in a taxi last night.

★★ **3** Write the correct form of the verbs.

A What's the most amazing newspaper story ¹*you've ever read* (you/ever read)?
B I ² .... (not read) very many, but I ³ .... (hear) a lot of stories from other people!
A For example?
B Well, it's the silly ones I remember the best. A player ⁴ .... (have) to stay in hospital with head injuries after a cricket match.
A What happened?
B He ⁵ .... (hit) the ball really hard, the ball ⁶ .... (go) up into the sky and ⁷ .... (kill) a passing duck.
A You're joking!
B No, no! And then the duck ⁸ .... (fall) out of the sky and ⁹ .... (strike) the player on the head!
A I don't believe it! That's the most amazing story anyone ¹⁰ .... (ever tell) me!
B Imagine that!

★★ **4** Complete the text with the correct form of these verbs.

receive	recommend	say	send
start	take	~~win~~	write

Local teen wins national blog contest

Elena Márquez, a 15-year-old from GBS High School, ¹ *has won* first prize in a national contest for school blogs. Elena ² .... writing the blog two years ago when she ³ .... a camera as a present. She ⁴ .... over a thousand photos of teenagers in the street, and she ⁵ .... a fashion report every month in that time. Her design teacher at school ⁶ .... that she enter the contest, and the organisers ⁷ .... her a text message last Monday to tell her about the prize. Her family ⁸ .... they are very proud of her.

Grammar Reference pages 92–93

Reading

1 **Read the text quickly and choose the best headline.**
   a Amusing pet monkeys
   b Man versus monkey
   c Winemaking in South Africa

AnimalNews.netcom

| HOME | NEWS | BLOG | FEATURES | PHOTOS |

....
by Wayne Chapman

There are many stories about conflicts between people and wild animals. We have heard about elephants in Africa eating village people's plants. There have also been reports of foxes living in people's gardens in the UK. As towns and cities use more and more land, animals have less land to live on. Usually it's the animals which lose the competition. But in some places the animals are slowly winning.

I've discovered an amazing story from South Africa. In one part of the country, people grow a lot of grapes for making wine. A few years ago, they began to have problems with large groups of monkeys which live in the mountains nearby. The monkeys love the sweet fruit. They ate all the grapes they wanted, and then ran off to the mountains to sleep. The farmers reacted angrily, but some people defended the monkeys. 'The monkeys have always lived here,' they said.

But recently, the monkeys have become difficult, because they get into people's homes to steal food. And they're not friendly like the monkeys on TV! One day, they even frightened a ten-year-old boy when he heard strange noises in the kitchen. People call the police, but they're not allowed to hurt the animals. So nowadays, many families are selling their homes and moving away.

Imagine that! If you have any good animal stories from your town, please send them to me!

2 **Complete the sentences with a word from the text.**
   1 Wild animals living near human beings often create *conflicts*.
   2 The problem is often the .... which humans use.
   3 The monkeys in South Africa enjoy eating ....
   4 The farmers were very .... with the monkeys.
   5 Nowadays, the monkeys are more ....
   6 Many people are .... of the monkeys, and sell their homes.

Listening

1 🔊 **19** **Listen to the recording and choose the best answer.**
The main subject of the interview is Steve Black's .... .

   a preferences in music
   b career as a musician
   c concert performances

2 🔊 **19** **Listen again and choose the correct option.**
   1 Steve Black plays the *guitar* / *drums*.
   2 His parents *played* / *didn't play* a lot of music.
   3 When he was at school, he was a *good* / *bad* student.
   4 He *writes* / *doesn't write* most of the lyrics.
   5 His group has recorded *six* / *sixteen* albums.

Writing A profile

1 **Find and correct the mistakes in these phrases. (S= spelling, G= grammar, P= punctuation)**

  1 wining tenis titles, and turned proffesional at fifteen   (S)

  winning tennis titles, and turned professional

  2 he did not lose his ability   (G)

  ....

  3 in 2008 he has also started a foundation   (G)

  ....

  4 which is one of the balearic islands in spain   (P)

  ....

2 **Read the text. Match the phrases (1–4) from Exercise 1 with the gaps (a–d).**

  Rafael Nadal is one of the greatest tennis players of all time. He was the first player to win the French Open seven times, and he is currently number 2 in the world. I admire him for his skill and his character, and also for the work he does through his foundation.

  Nadal was born in 1986 on the island of Mallorca, ª *.4.* . He went to school in his home town of Manacor. At the age of 12, he was already ᵇ.... . He did not move to Barcelona to train, but stayed in Manacor in order to finish school. In 2005 at the age of 19, he won his first French Open title.

  Nowadays he continues playing tennis and winning competitions, but ᶜ.... to help children and young people locally and abroad. In 2010 he visited different educational projects in India, to show his support for the projects and help other people become aware of them. Nadal has become internationally famous, but ᵈ.... to understand and help other people.

3 **Put these ideas in column A, according to the paragraph they appear in.**

achievements	career	conclusion
early life	education	~~introduction~~
recent activities	reasons for admiring	

	A Rafael Nadal's profile	B .... profile
Paragraph 1	*introduction*	
Paragraph 2		
Paragraph 3		

4 **Think of a person you would like to write about. Add information about that person to column B.**

5 **Write a profile of the person you have chosen in three paragraphs. Use your ideas and information from Exercises 3 and 4.**

  ....
  ....
  ....
  ....
  ....
  ....
  ....
  ....
  ....
  ....
  ....
  ....
  ....

5 Happy Holidays

Vocabulary Holidays

★ **1** Match the sentence beginnings (1–7) to the endings (a–g).

1 Do you eat out on holiday   *e*
2 I prefer to stay in hotels
3 We like to go camping
4 I've only seen a few sights
5 Do you often go abroad
6 We got lost in the city
7 She's written a travel blog

a or do you prefer holidays in your own country?
b and we don't mind what the weather's like.
c and had to take a taxi back.
d for her trip to Turkey.
e or do you cook in the apartment?
f because many of them are closed.
g but I can't usually afford to.

★★ **2** Complete the sentences with the correct form of these verbs.

book	buy	check into	get
~~lose~~	pack	put up	

1 Good morning! I'm afraid they've *lost* our luggage!
2 The weather was cold and cloudy, so he didn't .... a tan.
3 Dad, you should learn how to .... a tent before going on holiday!
4 Have you .... your bags for the trip?
5 Our neighbours have .... a two-week holiday in Portugal.
6 We .... the hotel and then went out for a walk.
7 How many souvenirs have you .... ?

★★ **3** Choose the correct options.

1 George and Mildred *went / booked* a holiday in the Caribbean.
2 They didn't usually *get / go* abroad, but this year was different.
3 They *put up / packed* their bags at home.
4 They had a good flight, but they *got lost / lost* their luggage.
5 So they didn't *go / see* the sights when they arrived.
6 Instead of *staying / buying* souvenirs, they had to *stay / buy* clothes!

★★ **4** Complete the conversation with these words

holiday	hotel	luggage	sights
~~souvenirs~~	tan	tent	

A So what was Ibiza like?
B Wonderful!
A Did you buy any [1] *souvenirs*?
B Just a few things for the family.
A Did you book the [2] .... or did you travel on your own?
B We went on our own. The idea was to go camping, but there was nowhere to put up a [3] ....
A What about the campsites?
B They were too busy, with too many people.
A So what did you do?
B We checked into a cheap [4] .... and stayed there.
A Did you see the [5] .... ?
B Not really! We just went to the beach and got a good [6] ....
A Yes, I noticed! So you had a good time?
B Yes, except that Derek lost his [7] .... on the way home!
A What a shame!

Vocabulary page 108

Reading

★ **1** Read the texts quickly and choose the best title.

    a Your adventure holidays

    b Your cheap holidays

    c Your family holidays

Brenda

In my family, we've been to the beach every summer since I was small. It's always been fun, because we live in a big city and the change is great! I love staying in a hotel because I don't have to make the bed, and we love eating out because my parents don't have to cook and I don't have to wash up afterwards! And we all enjoy getting a good tan. But the best of all is that my parents pay for the holidays!

Kieran

There are six of us in our family, so we've often had problems with holidays. But for the last five years, we've agreed together on where we want to go. Last year we booked a holiday abroad. Then when we got there, we decided to have time to see the sights in the city, time to go shopping for souvenirs and then free time for different activities. That way, we avoid a lot of silly arguments!

We're twin brothers, and we've had lots of different holidays with our parents. We've usually enjoyed them, too, except for museums and monuments, which are a bit boring. So this year, because we're already 16, our parents let us go camping with some friends, and it was brilliant. We did lots of walking and climbing, we didn't get lost and it wasn't expensive.

Rob and Doug

★ **2** Complete the sentences with the correct names.

    1 *Kieran* visited another country last year.

    2 .... had a new kind of holiday this year.

    3 .... usually goes to the beach.

    4 .... didn't go with the family this year.

    5 .... often goes to a hotel.

    6 ....'s family organises the way they spend their time.

★★ **3** Are the sentences true (T) or false (F)?

    1 Brenda lives in a small town.   *F*

    2 She often does chores at home.   ....

    3 Kieran's family can't always agree on what to do.   ....

    4 They had a lot of arguments last year.   ....

    5 The twins aren't very keen on museums and monuments.   ....

    6 They had quite a lazy holiday this year.   ....

Brain Trainer

Underline these adjectives in the texts in Exercise 1:

boring
silly
expensive
free
brilliant
different

Now do Exercise 1.

Grammar Present perfect + *for* and *since; How long?*

★ 1 Choose the correct options.

1 We've been here *for* / *since* six days.
2 She's read three books *for* / *since* we arrived.
3 They haven't been camping *for* / *since* 2012.
4 We haven't seen TV *for* / *since* a week!
5 I haven't stayed in a hotel *for* / *since* I was ten!
6 They haven't stopped dancing *for* / *since* three hours!
7 He hasn't written his travel blog *for* / *since* last weekend.

★ 2 Rewrite the sentences. Put *for* or *since* in the correct place.

1 My family has lived here ten years.
   My family has lived here for ten years.
2 I've studied at this school 2008.
   ....
3 Carrie and I have been friends we were kids.
   ....
4 We haven't seen Grandma a long time.
   ....
5 I've wanted a new bicycle six months.
   ....
6 She's had her pet dog last Christmas.
   ....

★★ 3 Complete the conversation with these words.

the end of	the last five weeks	the last two
the weekend	three years	~~your birthday~~

A Irene! I haven't seen you since ¹ *your birthday* in May! How are you?
B Fine thanks! And you? Where have you been for ² .... months?
A Oh, I've been abroad, you know. I had an exchange trip to Denmark. I've only been home again since ³ ....
B Did you have a good time?
A It was very interesting, yes. I've studied Danish for ⁴ .... now, so I was able to practise a lot! But what about you? What's new?
B I've been on holiday since ⁵ .... June, when school finished. And I've had a holiday job for ⁶ .... , so I'm earning a little money.
A That's wonderful! I'm very happy for you!

★★ 4 Write sentences to complete the postcard.

POSTCA

Hi Jackie!
Here we are in Italy! ¹ *We / be here / ten days*, and it's been great. ² *We / go / beach / every day / we arrived*, and the water's perfect. ³ *My parents / rent a car / five days*, so we're seeing the sights as well. I'm writing now from Venice. ⁴ *We / be / in the city / ten o'clock this morning*, and there are more tourists than local people! We're having a drink in a café, and ⁵ *I / write / five postcards / we sat down at the table*. I wanted to write a travel blog, of course, but ⁶ *I / be / too busy / the holiday started*, so you'll have to wait until we get back home before you see the photos. The holiday is a bit tiring, but ⁷ *I / not sleep / so well / a long time!*
Love,
Lucas

1 *We've been here for ten days.*
2 ....
3 ....
4 ....
5 ....
6 ....
7 ....

★ 5 Make questions for the underlined answers.

1 I've sent <u>twenty</u> text messages since this morning.
2 She's had her MP3 player <u>since Christmas</u>.
3 He's been on the plane <u>for four hours</u>.
4 They've driven <u>three hundred</u> kilometres today.
5 She hasn't got up early <u>for a week</u>!
6 We've been in the swimming pool <u>since two o'clock</u>.
7 He's caught <u>six</u> fish since lunchtime!

1 *How many text messages have you sent?*
2 ....
3 ....
4 ....
5 ....
6 ....
7 ....

Grammar Reference pages 94–95

Vocabulary Meanings of *get*

★ **1** Match these verbs to the meanings of *get* in the sentences (1–6). Use the correct forms.

arrive	buy	~~fetch~~	became	receive	walk

1 Can you get me some milk from the fridge?
fetch

2 I got this new top in the sales.
....

3 What time did you get home after the disco?
....

4 We got on the bus near the stadium.
....

5 When it got dark, we made a fire.
....

6 Did you get that watch for your birthday?
....

★ **2** Choose the correct meaning for the verb *get.*

1 I got a phone call from my friend.
fetched / (*received*)

2 We got off the bus opposite the station.
arrived at / walked

3 We got to the hotel about three o'clock.
bought / arrived at

4 It got cold in the room.
became / fetched

5 The receptionist got some blankets for us.
fetched / bought

6 We got some souvenirs the next morning.
bought / became

★ **3** Put the words in the correct order.

1 A this / school / you / get / did / to / morning / How / ?
How did you get to school this morning?
  B I took the bus.

2 A Why did you switch on the light?
  B frightened / the / Because / I / in / got / dark
....

3 A Have you seen my jacket anywhere?
  B you / moment / Yes, / it / for / in / I'll / a / get
....

4 A Did you have a good time at the market?
  B new / some / Yes, / I / shoes / got
....

5 A What happened to your friend?
  B train / He / the / got / disappeared / on / and / !
....

6 A message / Did / my / get / you / ?
....
  B What message? I haven't seen any messages!

★★ **4** Read the text. Replace *get* with the correct form of these verbs.

arrive at	become	buy	fetch	receive	~~walk~~

We ¹**got** off the train at a small station in the countryside, and walked to the campsite. It ²**was getting** dark, and we were tired from the journey. When we ³**got to** the campsite, it was difficult to see. We had to ⁴**get** a torch from the man in the small shop at the entrance and then went to put up the tent. Half an hour later, we were still trying, but we were lucky because we ⁵**got** some help from one of the other campers. Then we sent Gary to ⁶**get** some wood so we could light a fire.

1 *walked*
2 ....
3 ....
4 ....
5 ....
6 ....

Vocabulary page 108

Chatroom Asking for information

Speaking and Listening

★ **1** 🎧 20   Match the questions (1–6) to the answers (a–f). Then listen and check.

1 Excuse me! Can you help us?   *f*
2 Where's a good place to buy souvenirs?
3 Is there a good place to have coffee there?
4 How can we get there?
5 Is it far?
6 How long does it take to get to the bus station?

a It takes about ten minutes on foot.
b Yes, there's a nice little café on the corner.
c Not really. It's only about half a mile.
d There's a good shop opposite the museum.
e Well, you can walk or take a bus.
f Sure! What are you looking for?

★ **2**   🎧 21   Put the conversation in the correct order. Then listen and check.

a Is it far from here?   ....
b Oh, yes! That's next to the church in North Street.   ....
c Thanks very much!   ....
d Excuse me! Can you help me?   .1..
e It's about five minutes down that street over there.   ....
f Sure! What's the problem?   ....
g I'm looking for a restaurant called 'Cool Kitchen'.   ....

★★ **3**   🎧 22   Complete the conversation with these words. Then listen and check.

a~~ good place~~	can I get	go along this street
How long	on the left	the shopping centre

A Excuse me! Can you help me?
B Sure! What do you need?
A Is there ¹ *a good place* to buy camera batteries near here?
B There's a camera shop on Kings Road, but that's a bit far.
A ²....................... does it take to get there?
B It takes a while if you're walking.
A How about a big supermarket? They usually have batteries.
B OK! Yes, there's one in ³....................... down the road.
A How ⁴....................... there?
B It's about a ten minute walk.
A Great!
B OK. Well, ⁵....................... 'till you see a big church on the corner.
A All right.
B Then, cross the footbridge ⁶......................., and the shopping centre's on the other side of the river.
A That's super! Thanks very much.
B You're welcome!

★★ **4**   🎧 22   Listen to the conversation in Exercise 3 again. Choose the correct options.

1 There are (two) / three places to buy camera batteries.
2 Kings Road *is / isn't* near where the speakers are.
3 The camera shop *is / isn't* in the shopping centre.
4 Speaker A *is visiting / lives in* the town.
5 The shopping centre is *before / after* the footbridge.

★★ **5**   Write a conversation. Use phrases from Exercises 1–3 and this information:

An English-speaking tourist in your home town asks you about a good place to eat out. You recommend a restaurant and its location.

Speaking and Listening page 117

Grammar Present perfect with *just*

★ **1** Match the questions (1–6) to the answers (a–f).

1 What's the matter with Derek? *c*
2 Has anyone seen my glasses?
3 Is this the bus for Bristol?
4 Did I give you my mobile?
5 Are those my school papers?
6 Can I speak to Fiona, please?

a Sorry! I've just spilled water on them!
b Sorry, she's just gone out.
c He's just lost his luggage.
d I'm afraid you've just missed it.
e You've just sat on them, Grandma.
f No! You've just put it in your bag!

★ **2** Complete the sentences with the correct form of these verbs.

blow	go	lose	melt	put	~~use~~

1 Somebody has just *used* all the suntan lotion!
2 I've just .... my hotel key.
3 The wind has just .... my magazine into the pool!
4 We bought ice cream, but it's just .... !
5 Louis has just .... up the tent, and there's a bull in the field!
6 I've just .... shopping and I forgot the eggs.

★ **3** Put the words in the correct order.

1 travel / blog / just / I've / London / on / written / a
I've just written a travel blog on London.
2 prize / in / just / a / Lucy's / a / competition / won
....
3 bought / new / dad / just / Ken's / a / has / car
....
4 booked / a / Peter's / holiday / just / Germany / in
....
5 Canada / They've / come / camping / back / from / in / just
....
6 eaten / good / just / restaurant / a / very / out / at / We've
....

★★ **4** Look at the pictures. Write sentences using *just*.

1 *He's just fallen off his bike.*
2 ....
3 ....
4 ....
5 ....
6 ....

Grammar Reference pages 94–95

Reading

1 Read the text quickly. What kind of text is it?

    a a magazine article
    b a travel blog
    c a letter to the family

WEDNESDAY We're continuing our week in Amsterdam. Mum and Dad have gone to the Rijksmuseum, and we've just returned to the hotel from the Van Gogh Museum. It was modern and interesting. I liked the painting of his shoes, but Clara says the picture of the yellow house is her favourite. We've also been to a huge street market, where we bought some souvenirs.

THURSDAY We've been up since seven o'clock this morning because we've been on an excursion to visit a real windmill. It was made of wood and was really pretty on the outside, but full of spiders' webs on the inside. It was really old, but it still worked! We had lunch in a little town before coming back to the city. (Did you know the Dutch have mayonnaise with their chips?!)

And this afternoon we went for a walk in one of the big parks. I've never seen so many flowers!

FRIDAY Tomorrow's our last day here. This morning we went to see Anne Frank's house, because I read the book at school last year and I wanted to see it for myself. It made me think about how lucky I am. Anyway, we're eating out tonight at an Indonesian restaurant, so tomorrow's blog post will be about exotic food!

2 Choose the correct options.

    1 The writer *visited /* (*didn't visit*) the Rijksmuseum.
    2 They went shopping on *Wednesday / Thursday*.
    3 The windmill *was / wasn't* very clean inside.
    4 On Thursday afternoon, they *went out of / stayed in* the hotel.
    5 For the writer, Anne Frank's house was *boring / interesting*.

Listening

1 🔊 **23** **Listen and choose the correct options.**

    1 The speaker is going to have (*Chinese*) */ Indian / Italian* food.
    2 He and his friend have eaten a lot of *fast food / pizzas / sandwiches* this week.
    3 The woman says lunch at the restaurant costs *€6 / €15 / €16*.
    4 The restaurant is *takeaway / self-service / waiter service*.
    5 The woman *explains how to get there / shows them the way on a map / takes them there herself*.

2 🔊 **23** **Who says these phrases? Listen again and write B for the boy or W for the woman.**

    1 What kind of food   *W*
    2 every day this week   ....
    3 I've been there   ....
    4 what's a buffet lunch?   ....
    5 you get the food yourself   ....
    6 Come with me   ....

Writing A travel guide

1 **Complete the text with these adjectives.**

fantastic	helpful	~~historic~~
musical	popular	sunny

One of my favourite holiday places is the ¹*historic* city of Stirling in central Scotland. It's not too big, it's got lots of good shops and restaurants, and the people are friendly and ²....................... . Summer is the best time to visit, when the weather's bright and ³....................... .

There are lots of things to see and do in and around Stirling. The castle is the most famous and ⁴....................... attraction. You can visit all of it, and it's interactive: you can wear medieval clothes, try the ⁵....................... instruments and smell the spices they cooked with. You can even sit in the king's chair in the Great Hall! And there are ⁶....................... views from the top. For day trips, you can visit a safari park, go walking in the hills, go fishing in the river, play golf and other sports or watch the Highland Games.

Stirling is easy to get to by car, bus or train. Check it out on the internet!

2 **Complete the chart with adjectives from the text. Then write more adjectives you remember.**

places	*historic*
people	
weather	
tourist attractions	

3 **Complete column A with ideas from the text in Exercise 1.**

	A Stirling	B My favourite holiday desination: ....
Introduction: Where is it? What are the people like? When is the best time to visit and why?	*Central Scotland*	
What is there to see and do?		
Conclusion: How can you get there? Where can you get more information?		

4 **Add ideas for your own favourite holiday destination to column B.**

5 **Write a travel guide in three paragraphs. Use your ideas and the adjectives and phrases from Exercises 2, 3 and 4.**

....
....
....
....
....
....
....
....
....
....
....
....

6 That's Life!

Vocabulary Household chores

★ **1** Match the verbs (1–8) to the nouns (a–h).

1	clear	a	the floor
2	do	b	the rubbish
3	feed	c	the washing machine
4	sweep	d	the car
5	make	e	the table
6	run	f	the cat
7	take out	g	the ironing
8	wash	h	your bed

★★ **2** Complete the sentences with the correct form of these verbs.

cook	do	hang out	lay
load	mow	vacuum	~~walk~~

1 Who's going to *walk* the dog this afternoon?
2 It's raining! Did you .... the washing this morning?
3 You .... the dishwasher, but you didn't switch it on!
4 Is it your turn to .... lunch today?
5 People don't .... the lawn in winter!
6 Could you .... the table for six, please?
7 I .... the washing-up yesterday!
8 Have you .... the carpet yet?

★★ **3** Choose the correct options.

1 Breakfast is finished! We need someone to *lay / clear* the table!
2 Jonathan! Have you *made / done* your bed yet?
3 No brushes please! It's much better to *sweep / vacuum* the floor.
4 It's stopped raining. You can *run / hang* out the washing now!
5 Here's the clean washing. Whose turn is it to *make / do* the ironing?
6 Mum! Don't go away without *laying / loading* the dishwasher!
7 Angela! I need you to *hang out / take out* the rubbish, please!
8 Herbert is going to *mow / vacuum* the lawn.

★★ **4** Use the information in the chart to write complete sentences.

George's chore list

1 *George has cleared the table.*
2 ....
3 ....
4 ....
5 ....
6 ....
7 ....
8 ....

Vocabulary page 109

Reading

★ **1**   **Match the names (1–3) to the number of people in their families (a–c).**

1 Becca   **a** four
2 Malcolm   **b** seven
3 Richie   **c** two

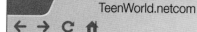

TeenWorld.netcom

← → C ♠

Teens and chores

On the subject of teenagers and household chores, we asked:
What happens in your home? Here are some of the answers you sent us.

Becca

I don't have to do very much at home because we have a cleaner who does most of the chores. But my mum says I must learn some things, so I make my own bed every day. She also says I must look after my pets, so I feed the cat and walk the dog in the afternoon. But I don't have to do the washing-up or anything because that's what dishwashers are for!

Malcolm

My sister and I have to help with the chores. My parents have a chart on the fridge door and every week we change activities. This week I must load and unload the dishwasher and my sister has to lay and clear the table. But she's five years younger than me, so I often have to do more than her. She never has to mow the lawn, for example, or do the ironing.

Richie

There are five children in our family and our parents tell us we must do our share of the housework. The older children have to do things like cook meals and take out the rubbish. The younger ones have to do smaller chores like clear the table and load the dishwasher.

★ **2**   **Choose the correct options.**

1 *Becca /* *Malcolm* does a lot of chores.
2 *Malcolm / Richie* does more than his younger sister.
3 *Becca / Richie* has to look after animals.
4 Only members of the family do the chores in *Becca's / Malcolm's* home.
5 The younger children usually do the easier chores in *Richie's / Becca's* home.

★★ **3**   **Complete the sentences.**

1 Becca has to do *some* chores every day.
2 Becca doesn't have to do the ....
3 Malcolm can see his chores on the ....
4 Malcolm's sister doesn't have to do .... chores.
5 Richie gives .... examples of the chores for the children in his house.

Grammar *have to/don't have to*   *must/mustn't*

★ 1 Read the chart. Are the sentences true (T) or false (F)?

	Millie	Mark
make the bed	✓	✓
do the ironing	✗	✓
run the washing machine	✗	✗
cook a meal	✓	✓
walk the dog	✓	✗
mow the lawn	✗	✗
wash the car	✗	✓
clear the table	✓	✗

1 Millie has to do more chores than Mark.   *F*
2 Millie and Mark both have to make the bed.   ....
3 Only Millie has to do the ironing.   ....
4 Mark doesn't have to run the washing machine.   ....
5 Millie doesn't have to cook a meal.   ....
6 Mark has to walk the dog.   ....
7 Millie and Mark don't have to mow the lawn.   ....
8 Millie has to clear the table.   ....

★★ 2 Complete the questions with the correct form of the verbs. Add the correct verb in the answers.

1 *Do you have to* (you/have to) clear the table? No, I *don't*.
2 .... (your brother/have to) sweep the floor? Yes, he ....
3 .... (your parents/have to) share the chores? Yes, they ....
4 .... (your sister/have to) take out the rubbish? No, she ....
5 .... (you/have to) cook meals? Yes, I ....

★★ 3 Complete the conversation with the correct form of *have to*.

A What kind of chores ¹ *do you have to* (you) do at the summer camp?
B I ² .... make my bed every morning.
A And outside your room? ³ .... (you) work in the kitchen?
B No, I don't. The kitchen staff ⁴ .... load and unload the dishwasher, and they also ⁵ .... take the rubbish out.
A What about your clothes?
B We ⁶ .... run the washing machines because the supervisors do that, but we ⁷ .... hang out the washing.

★ 4 Read the sentences. Write O for Obligation, N/O for No obligation or P for Prohibition.

1 You must do the washing-up after breakfast!   *O*
2 We mustn't feed the cat more than once a day.   ....
3 I must make the bed before going to school.   ....
4 We don't have to cook meals on weekdays.   ....
5 My brother must walk the dog every morning.   ....
6 Joanna doesn't have to do the ironing every day.   ....
7 You mustn't wash the car in the street.   ....

★★ 5 Look at the rules for students sharing a flat. Write sentences with *must/mustn't*, *have to/don't have to*.

Students' rules

① take out the rubbish before six o'clock   P
② run the washing machine in the morning   O
③ hang out the washing on the balcony   P
④ do the ironing in the kitchen   N/O
⑤ vacuum the floor at night   P
⑥ sweep the floor on the landing   O
⑦ feed the neighbour's cats   N/O

1 *We mustn't take out the rubbish before six o'clock.*
2 ....
3 ....
4 ....
5 ....
6 ....
7 ....

Grammar Reference pages 96–97

Vocabulary Feelings adjectives

★ **1** Complete the definitions with these adjectives.

confident	confused	embarrassed	fed up
grateful	guilty	upset	

1 When someone has solved a problem for you, you feel *grateful*.
2 When you do something wrong and don't admit it, you feel ....
3 When you make a big mistake in front of other people, you feel ....
4 When you know for sure that you can do something well, you feel ....
5 When you don't know what to do and can't make a decision, you feel ....
6 When other people do nothing and you have to do everything, you feel ....
7 When a good friend has a lot of bad luck, you feel ....

★★ **2** Put the letters in the correct order to complete the text.

FEBRUARY 24

Tuesday

Another day of ups and downs! Ewan appeared today with a new smartphone, which is much better than mine – I felt so ¹ *jealous* (asleujo)! And I got my Maths exam marks back: 6.5. I was a bit ² .... (depositpinda) because I studied a lot and I expected a higher mark. But Stella got an 8, which is brilliant, so I felt really ³ .... (dalg) for her. She was very ⁴ .... (rovenus) the day before the exam because her parents promised her some concert tickets if she passed. So she's been happy and ⁵ .... (eladrex) all day! Then in the library this afternoon, I was feeling a bit ⁶ .... (yellon) because Toby wasn't there. Stella said he was in trouble, because she saw him outside the principal's office, so I got worried. But then Toby appeared. It was only a message, so I felt ⁷ .... (liedreve) that there was nothing wrong.

★★ **3** Choose the correct options.

1 Our team have won their last three matches, so they're *confused / confident* about winning tomorrow.
2 I'm *fed up / nervous* with waiting for the bus. I think I'll just walk instead!
3 Janet got very *guilty / upset* the other day when she lost her mobile phone.
4 Nelson is a bit *jealous / confused* because my bike has better brakes than his.
5 I fell over in class and everyone laughed! I felt really *disappointed / embarrassed*.
6 I lost my address book at the weekend, but Saskia found it, so I felt *relieved / relaxed*.
7 When the Science teacher asked about the water on the curtains, Tommy looked a bit *guilty / grateful*.

★★ **4** Complete the conversation with these words.

confused	embarrassed	fed up	grateful
lonely	relaxed	upset	

A Did you see the TV show last night? The one about the friends who share a flat?
B Yes, but I got a bit ¹ *confused* because the story wasn't very clear. Who was the boy that got ² .... because someone spilt coffee on his laptop?
A That was Adam. In general, he's ³ .... with his flatmates because he's tidy and organised, and they're not! Their way of doing things is much more ⁴ ....
B You mean careless! So who was the girl whose face went so red?
A That was Nikki. She was ⁵ .... because she got Thierry's name wrong, and the others laughed. And that's why she was so ⁶ .... to Lucas for helping her.
B OK, now I understand better. Do you often watch it?
A Whenever I'm feeling a bit ⁷ .... , I watch another episode. It's great!
B Cool.

> **Vocabulary** page 109

 **Giving advice**

Speaking and Listening

★ **1** 🔊 **24** **Match the problems (1–6) to the advice (a–f). Then listen and check.**

1 I've been a bit lonely recently.   *d*
2 I'm tired of the same cereals!
3 I spend too much time on the internet.
4 I miss my brother who's in the UK.
5 I don't get the presents I want.
6 I have to clean my room every week.

a I don't think you should complain. It only takes ten minutes!
b Maybe you should buy them yourself!
c Why don't you video call him?
d Maybe you should call your friends!
e Why don't you have toast, then?
f I think you should do more outdoor activities.

★ **2** 🔊 **25** **Put the words in the correct order to make answers. Then listen and check.**

1 A I'm not sure this T-shirt fits me very well.
   B size / try / you / Why / different / a / don't / ?
   Why don't you try a different size?

2 A I'd like to learn how to draw well.
   B drawing / you / classes / go / Maybe / to / should.
   ....

3 A I'm thinking of changing the colour of my hair.
   B that / I / worry / don't / you / should / think / about / !
   ....

4 A I want to eat more healthily.
   B shouldn't / meals / Maybe / have / between / you / snacks / !
   ....

5 A I need more pocket money.
   B chores / you / home / should / do / think / more / at / I / first / !
   ....

6 A There's no room in my wardrobe for all my clothes!
   B new / I / should / many / think / clothes / don't / buy / so / you
   ....

★★ **3** 🔊 **26** **Complete the conversation with these words. Then listen and check.**

| a bit fed up | I don't think | I feel tired |
| Why don't you | you don't have time | You should |

A You're looking ¹ *a bit fed up*! What's the matter?
B I have to get up too early for school so ²......................... all the time.
A Well, ³......................... you should go to bed so late!
B And I hate having to wear school uniform. Why can't I wear my own clothes?
A ⁴......................... think about more important things?
B Like what?
A Like helping me with the chores! When you're busy working, ⁵......................... to worry about anything else.
B Yes, but I have to study. And I get good marks at school!
A So you've got nothing to worry about. ⁶......................... learn to wake up with a smile!

★★ **4** 🔊 **26** **Listen to the conversation in Exercise 3 again. Complete the sentences with one word.**

1 Speaker B always feels *tired*.
2 Speaker B doesn't like .... a uniform.
3 Speaker A's opinions are .... from Speaker B's opinions.
4 Speaker A says it's more important to .... things than to worry.
5 Speaker A says that B should .... to be more positive in the morning.

★★ **5** **Write a conversation. Use expressions from Exercises 1–3, and this information:**

A friend tells you about a problem. Give him/her advice. Mention two things you think they should do and two things you think they shouldn't do.

Speaking and Listening page 118

Grammar Predictions with *will, won't, might*

★ 1 **Choose the correct options.**

1 I don't think our visitors *will* / *might* arrive on time.
2 They're not sure about the weather. They *will* / *might* stay at home instead.
3 She's a Bieber fan! She *will* / *might* go to the Bieber concert!
4 He doesn't read. He *won't* / *might not* pass his literature exam.
5 We haven't decided. We *will* / *might* go to visit Elaine's family.
6 School is closed today. There *won't* / *might not* be anyone in the office.
7 Shane's a bit confused. He *will* / *might* study to be a mechanic.

★ 2 **Match the questions (1–6) to the answers (a–f).**

1 Do you think our team will win?   *e*
2 Do you think she'll come to the party?
3 Do you think it will rain tomorrow?
4 Will John like his present?
5 Will Emma be glad to see me?
6 Will we get to the station in time?

a I know she will!
b With this traffic, I don't think we will.
c I don't know! He might not.
d She might, but she's working late today.
e I'm sure they will.
f I don't think it will. It's too sunny.

★★ 3 **Complete the sentences with *will*, *won't* or *might*.**

1 Uncle Tom's in China so he *won't* be here tomorrow.
2 The hotel's next to a park so it .... be very quiet.
3 The flight is on time so Dad .... arrive in ten minutes.
4 I don't know what time they close so they .... still be open.
5 The trains are very busy today so you .... not get a ticket.
6 He's tired and nervous so he .... be very happy if you make a noise.

★★ 4 **Make sentences.**

1 our team / not win / because / not train / hard enough.   (won't)
   Our team won't win because they haven't trained hard enough.
2 Leonor / come / because / miss / bus.   (won't)
   ....
   ....
3 Jack / not want / talk / because / very upset. (might)
   ....
   ....
4 Grandfather / be disappointed / if you / not send him / a letter.   (will)
   ....
   ....
5 Chris / be embarrassed / if Sheena / tell / that story!   (might)
   ....
   ....
6 Tony / listen / you / because / too jealous. (won't)
   ....
   ....
7 Tina / not play / on Saturday / because / got a cold.   (might)
   ....
   ....

Grammar Reference pages 96–97

Reading

1 Read the text quickly. Match the writers to their opinions.

1 Caitlin   **a** pessimist
2 Brendan   **b** optimist

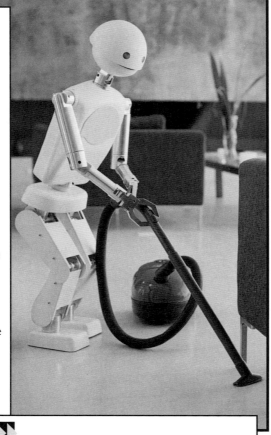

Homes of the future

← → C ⌂

HOME   NEWS   COMMENTS   FEATURES   PHOTOS

Send us your comments on the article 'Homes of the future'! ▶▶

Caitlin says ▶▶

I feel confident that we'll have robots to do all the chores! I'm fed up having to do the ironing and take out the rubbish. I've seen Japanese robots on TV, so I think we might have domestic robots soon. For example, my friend's mum has just bought a machine that vacuums the floor by itself. If you don't have to do chores, there's more time to study – and have fun. I also think homes will be much greener, because the buildings will be better and they'll use clean electricity from the sun and things like that.

Brendan says ▶▶

I don't think homes will be so different in the future. Some people might have robots, in the same way that some people now have cleaning and gardening staff in their houses, but most people will still have to do their own chores. Robots will make you lazy. What will people do with all the extra time? Play more video games? There's nothing wrong with doing a few chores every day: we should all be able to cook and clean, for example. And I'm not sure about greener homes. Maybe some new homes, but not older ones, because people might not have the money to modernise them. In short, I don't think we should expect very big changes.

2 Are the sentences true (T) or false (F)?

1 Caitlin doesn't like doing chores.   *T*
2 Brendan doesn't mind doing chores.   ....
3 Caitlin's friend has to vacuum her home.   ....
4 Brendan doesn't think there will be so many robots.   ....
5 Caitlin thinks people won't have to study so much.   ....
6 Brendan thinks that all homes will be much more modern.   ....

Listening

1 🔊 27 Listen and complete the summary of the conversation.

The caller's name is ¹ *Max*. He's worried about his ² .... who is going to university. He says he'll ³ .... her because there are no other ⁴ .... at home. The programme presenter says the boy should be more ⁵ .... She says it's a good ⁶ .... to talk, but that the boy shouldn't forget his ⁷ .... from ⁸ ....

2 🔊 27 Match the expression beginnings (1–5) to the endings (a–e). Then listen again and check.

1 give you   *c*
2 going away   ....
3 very lonely   ....
4 any other   ....
5 it's great   ....

a brothers or sisters
b to keep in touch
c some advice
d without her
e to university

Writing A problem page

1 Rewrite the sentences using *because* or *so*.

1 I can't buy a mobile phone because I don't have enough money.   (so)
I don't have enough money so I can't buy a mobile phone.

2 They've got a dishwasher so she doesn't have to do the washing-up.   (because)

....
....

3 You shouldn't get so upset because all friends argue sometimes!   (so)

....
....

4 I can't hang out the washing because it's raining!   (so)

....
....

5 Everyone's gone home so I'm feeling a bit lonely.   (because)

....
....

6 I can't do so many chores because I have to study!   (so)

....
....

2 Read the problem and the advice. Answer the questions.

1 How many reasons with *because* are there?
2 How many results with *so*?

3 Complete column A with details from Elvira's reply.

	A Elvira's reply	B Your reply
Paragraph 1 General advice	Recommendation:	
Paragraph 2 Specific ideas	1 show .... 2 explain .... 3 show .... 4 Mum talk	
Paragraph 3 Ending	Two things to remember: 5 .... 6	

4 Read the following problem. In column B, write your ideas for a reply.

All my friends have smartphones, so they can send each other messages all the time. I haven't got one, because my parents say I don't need one, and also because they say they're expensive. I would like them to change their mind! What should I do?
Alex

5 Now write your reply to Alex in three paragraphs. Use your ideas and information from Exercises 3 and 4.

Most of my friends at school have an account on a social network, so they're always in touch. They all know what everyone is doing – except me. I'm fed up because I can't talk to my friends or share photos with them! My mum says that it can be dangerous. But nothing has ever happened to my friends! What should I do?

Bethany

Problem page

Elvira says:

Right, Bethany. Yes, that happens to a lot of teenagers nowadays, so we have some ideas to help you. But remember you mustn't get upset, because for many parents social networks are totally new!

The first thing you should do is sit down at the computer with your mum and show her the network because she might not feel very confident about it. And if she doesn't use a computer very often, she won't know how the system works so you'll have to explain that as well. Maybe you know other members of the family – cousins, for example – who are also in the network. Show your mum their photos, their account, and how long they've used the network. Then she should talk to your aunt or uncle, so she can see she doesn't have to worry about you. Then she'll feel more relaxed.

Finally, don't forget your own responsibilities: keep your passwords secret and don't accept people you don't know as friends.

Check Your Progress 2

Grammar

1 **Complete the conversations with the Present perfect form of these verbs.**

come back	go	have to
hear	~~not see~~	stay

A Hi, Jan! **0** *I haven't seen* you for a while! How are you?
B Fine, thanks!
A You're looking very tanned! **1** .... (you) to the beach?
B Yes! We **2** .... (just) from the coast. It was great!
A How long did you stay?
B Ten days. What about you?
A I **3** .... at home since school finished. My parents **4** .... work this month, but we're going to London next week! Have you been there?
B No, but I **5** .... about it from friends who have been. It sounds like fun.
A I'll send you a postcard!
B OK!

know	meet	move	not talk	not write

A Who was that?
B That was my friend Ben. I **6** .... to him for ages! We used to be neighbours.
A How long **7** .... him?
B Since we lived in the old part of town. Why?
A His face looks familiar. I think I **8** .... him.
B When was that?
A At Joanna's party last month. He was with some other boys I know.
B Joanna? Tom said I should send her an email, and I **9** .... it yet.
A You should do it soon then because she **10** .... (just) to another school.
B I didn't know that! Tell me more …

/ 10 marks

2 **Choose the correct options.**

0 The teacher says we (don't have to) / mustn't buy new trainers. We can use the ones from last year.

1 The school rules say that we *don't have to / mustn't* use mobile phones in class.

2 It's not necessary for you to wait. You *don't have to / mustn't* wait.

3 You can't wear a T-shirt here. You *have to / mustn't* wear a shirt and tie.

4 If you drive in England, remember that you *must / don't have to* drive on the left!

5 Uniforms in this school aren't essential. You *don't have to / mustn't* wear a uniform.

6 I'm afraid cameras aren't allowed in here! You *don't have to / mustn't* use a camera here.

7 She *will / might* be at our school, but I'm not very sure.

8 It's 14.30. Tom finishes work at 15.00, so he *won't / might* be at home now.

9 Don't worry, Mum! I promise I *'ll / might* call you when I get to the station.

10 I don't know if there's another bus. I *won't / might* have to stay the night.

/ 10 marks

Vocabulary

3 **Choose the correct options.**

0 When was the last time you .... camping?
  a got   **b** did   **c** went

1 Did you .... your tan at the beach or at the swimming pool?
  a book   **b** get   **c** go

2 Have you .... your bags yet?
  a packed   **b** checked into   **c** put up

3 Isn't it your turn to .... the washing this week?
  a clear   **b** run   **c** hang out

4 Oh no! I forgot to .... the dishwasher last night.
  a mow   **b** load   **c** sweep

5 Could you please .... the dog? It hasn't been out today!
  a do   **b** vacuum   **c** walk

/ 5 marks

4 Choose the correct options.

Did you hear the [0] *report* / *blog* / *newspaper* on the radio this morning? They were talking about this 15-year-old girl who was walking down the street when two men ran out of a shop in front of her. Two seconds later, a shop assistant appeared, screaming [1] *happily* / *hard* / *loudly* for help. The girl was [2] *lonely* / *confused* / *guilty* for a moment, but then ran after the men! She followed them along the street and round a corner, and saw them get into a car. She wrote down the car number [3] *carefully* / *carelessly* / *sadly* and went back to the shop. The shop assistant called the police and the men were arrested later that day. The shop owner was so [4] *disappointed* / *fed up* / *grateful* that he gave the girl a reward. You see? The interesting stories aren't just on the [5] *international news* / *journalists* / *news presenters*!

/ 5 marks

Speaking

5 Complete the conversations with these words/phrases.

an argument	I don't think you should
joking	Maybe you should try
strange	Why don't you

A Jared and I had [0] *an argument* last night.
B That's [1] .... You two have always been good friends.
A Yes, I know. But he wants to date me.
B You're [2] .... !
A No, seriously! And I'm not sure about what to do.
B Well, he's a really nice guy. [3] .... going out with him.
A Yes, but it might not work.
B [4] .... worry about that.
A But I don't want to lose a good friend!
B [5] .... take the weekend to make a decision?
A That's a good idea!

get there	How long does it take	Is it far
to buy souvenirs	We're looking for	

A Excuse me! Can you help us?
B Sure! What would you like to know?
A [6] .... the Science Museum. How can we [7] .... ?
B Well, you can walk or take a bus.
A [8] .... ?
B It's about two miles.
A [9] .... to get there?
B For healthy young people like you, about 15 minutes!
A And is there a good place [10] .... there?
B Yes, the museum has its own shop, and it's not too expensive.
A So, which way do we go?

/ 10 marks

Translation

6 Translate the sentences.

1 I'm afraid the 6.30 bus has just left!
....
2 I don't think you're allowed to put up tents in this area.
....
3 You don't have to come with us if you don't want to.
....
4 Would you mind doing the washing-up tonight?
....
5 You won't find any mosquitoes here. It's too cold!
....

/ 5 marks

Dictation

7 🔊 28 Listen and write.

1 ....
2 ....
3 ....
4 ....
5 ....

/ 5 marks

Vocabulary Protest and support

★ **1** Match these words to the definitions (1–6).

banner	~~charity~~
fundraising event	march
placard	volunteer

1 A non-commercial organisation that helps people in difficulty. *charity*
2 A walk by a large group of people, usually to make a protest. ....
3 A large notice with a message on it, usually carried on a stick. ....
4 A person who offers to work without receiving money. ....
5 An activity that people organise in order to collect money. ....
6 A long piece of cloth with a message on it. ....

★ **2** Match the sentence beginnings (1–6) to the endings (a–f).

1 Would you like to sign   *e*
2 We invite you to take part
3 We're having a collection
4 Would you like to make
5 Can you think of a good
6 Are you coming to the sit-in

a for the homeless people in our town.
b slogan about animal protection?
c a donation to save tigers?
d at the local theatre?
e our petition for safer schools?
f in the demonstration, on Sunday at 12 o'clock.

★★ **3** Choose the correct options.

1 Andrea is a *banner /* (*volunteer*) with a children's charity.
2 That placard has a very clever *donation / slogan* on it!
3 Our school is having a *donation / fundraising event* this weekend.
4 We've got a *collection / petition* with 50,000 signatures!
5 The *march / sit-in* starts at the station and finishes at the town hall.
6 Don't miss the *demonstration / donation* in the park at nine o'clock!

★★ **4** Complete the text with these words.

donation	march	petition	placards	~~sit-in~~	slogans

Support our miners' [1] *sit-in* at the coal mine!
They've been underground for 23 days now!

You can help by:

○ signing our [2] .... for better conditions
○ making a [3] .... to the support fund
○ taking part in Saturday's [4] .... from the town centre to the mine
○ writing [5] .... for Saturday's banners
○ making [6] .... for Saturday (we provide boards and sticks!)

Vocabulary page 110

Reading

★ **1 Read the text. Match the headings (A–D) to the paragraphs (1–4).**

A What can you do?   **B** What do we do?   **C** Why do we exist?   **D** Who are we?

Integration Now

1 *D*

We're called 'Integration Now', and we're a local charity that works to help immigrants to adapt to local life. But we would also like local people to meet immigrants, ᵃ*3*, and share their cultures and traditions – without banners, without slogans. We believe that life together is going to be richer and more fun that way.

2 ....

We're here because when you move to another country, it can be very difficult to adapt. You will probably have language problems; you'll often have to ᵇ.... ; your children will go to schools with children from different communities. Even the food ᶜ.... ! So we'd like to help people integrate into their new community.

3 ....

We're a group of volunteers who work from a small office. We give information and advice to immigrants. We take part in local events so that local people can ᵈ.... . Our food festivals are especially popular! And we organise language exchange sessions: you can help people learn your own language, and they will teach you some of theirs. Next year ᵉ.... to a bigger space for our own events.

4 ....

You don't have to give donations! Come and ᶠ.... with us. Meet some interesting people. You'll always learn something new!

★ **2 Match the phrases (1–6) to the gaps (a–f) in the text.**

1 ask for help   ....
2 meet immigrants   ....
3 get to know them   .*a*.
4 spend some time   ....
5 we're going to move   ....
6 will be different   ....

★★ **3 Are the sentences true (T) or false (F)?**

1 'Integration Now' works with both immigrants and local people.   *T*
2 They organise lots of marches and protests.   ....
3 They mention four common problems for immigrants.   ....
4 They work in a local school.   ....
5 Not many people go to the food festivals.   ....
6 It's not important to help by giving money.   ....

Grammar *be going to*

★ **1** **Match the questions (1–6) to the answers (a–f).**

1 Is John going to sign the petition?   c
2 Are you going to join the march?
3 Are your parents going to make placards?
4 What are you going to do with your old laptop?
5 Where's Ted going to study journalism?
6 When are you going to leave school?

a He wants to go to Liverpool.
b I'll leave at the end of my fourth year.
c He says he is.
d Yes, I am. Definitely!
e I'll probably give it to my cousin.
f Yes, they're going to make six of them.

★ **2** **Put the words in the correct order.**

1 A birthday / for / going / What / do / are / to / you / your / ?
What are you going to do for your birthday?
B I'll probably have a party.

2 A present / What's / to / next / Tamara / going / ?
....
....
B I think it's a report on sports.

3 A teacher / going / exams / When's / the / to / Maths / correct / the / ?
....
....
B She said she'll correct them next week.

4 A collection / Where / make / are / they / to / a / going / ?
....
....
B They'll probably do it in the high street.

5 A write / are / slogan / for / going / we / to / What / a / ?
....
....
B I'm not sure. Let's think of something original!

6 A invite / Who / you / to / for / are / the / going / weekend / ?
....
....
B A few of my good friends.

★★ **3** **Make questions for the underlined answers.**

1 We're going to organise <u>a fundraising event</u>.
What are you going to organise?
2 It's going to be <u>in the community centre</u>.
....
3 It's going to start <u>on Saturday at five o'clock</u>.
....
4 <u>Johnny Depp</u>'s going to be there.
....
5 We're going to have <u>a poster competition</u>.
....
6 <u>Our Science teacher</u>'s going to do a video report.
....

will or *be going to*

★ **4** **Choose the correct options.**

1 I've read the menu, and *I'll /(I'm going to)* have the fish.
2 It's Candice's birthday soon. Maybe *we'll / we're going to* get her a present.
3 He's too tired to cook, so *he'll / he's going to* order a takeaway.
4 Susan said *she'll probably / she's probably going to* come shopping with me.
5 They've bought the tickets. After the concert, their parents *will / are going to* pick them up.
6 She's not sure. Perhaps *she'll / she's going to* leave in the morning.

★★ **5** **Complete the conversation with the correct form of *will* or *going to*.**

A Have you got any plans for next week?
B On Tuesday, my dad and I ¹ *are going to* watch the football on TV. And on Friday, we ² .... probably go fishing, but that depends on the weather. What about you?
A The sales start on Monday, so my mum ³ .... buy me some new clothes. Then on Friday there's a concert.
B Who ⁴ .... play at the concert?
A A local group. One of my friends plays the drums.
B Wow! What else are you doing?
A I'm not sure. There's a circus in town this week, so maybe I ⁵ .... go there. And you?
B I can't go out much. I've got an exam on Thursday, so I ⁶ .... study for that.

Grammar Reference pages 98–99

Vocabulary Verb + preposition

★ **1 Choose the correct options.**

1 We're going to the demonstration because we don't *agree with* / *argue against* the new law.
2 I really *believe in* / *care about* the environment.
3 We haven't *decided on* / *worried about* a good slogan yet.
4 Ana is *hoping for* / *knows about* her interview to go well.
5 We think the factory should *apologise for* / *protest against* causing this pollution!
6 I'm joining the sit-in because I *disapprove of* / *decide on* the new uniforms.

★ **2 Match the sentence beginnings (1–6) to the endings (a–f).**

1 I'm afraid I can't agree   *e*
2 Mike should apologise
3 Anyone who cares
4 It's difficult to decide
5 I don't know anything
6 We're here to protest

a against the plans for another factory in our town.
b about melting ice in the Arctic.
c for his silly comments.
d about sea life should join the march.
e with your ideas about teenagers.
f on the best place for a day trip.

Brain Trainer

Match these verbs and prepositions:

insist	about
believe	on
worry	in

Now do Exercise 3.

★★ **3 Complete the conversation with the correct form of these verbs.**

| agree | believe | disapprove | insist | ~~protest~~ | worry |

A Hi! What are you ¹*protesting* against?
B We don't ².......................... with the council's plan to enforce a weekend curfew for teenagers.
A Really? I haven't heard about that.
B They're ³.......................... on 10 p.m. as the latest possible time for teenagers to be out!
A Is that right? I don't think that's really necessary.
B Well they say they ⁴.......................... about all the noise for the neighbours. They say they ⁵.......................... in everyone's right to relax at the weekend and therefore teenagers should be home before 10 p.m.
A Have you got a petition that I can sign?
B Sure! We've got a petition for anyone who ⁶.......................... of the curfew to sign.

★★ **4 Complete the text with the correct prepositions.**

We're planning a march for next Saturday, and we're hoping ¹*for* at least 5,000 people to join us. The council wants to build a new rubbish dump in the countryside. But we don't believe ².......................... dumps. We prefer to recycle all the rubbish. And we worry ³.......................... the plan, because that area is where many of us go on outings at the weekend. Our representatives have argued ⁴.......................... them for weeks now, but they insist ⁵.......................... going ahead with the project. So now is the time to show them how many of us disapprove ⁶.......................... their idea. They must understand how much we care ⁷.......................... our environment!

Vocabulary page 110

 **Persuading**

Speaking and Listening

★ 1 🔊 **29** **Match the comments (1–6) to the replies (a–f). Then listen and check.**

1 Let's go to a demonstration! Come on, it'll be fun. *c*
2 Why don't we join a march? I'm sure you'd enjoy it.
3 Are you coming to the sit-in with us? It's better than sitting at home.
4 How about making a collection for cancer research? Come on, it'll be fun.
5 Let's go to a fundraising event! I'm sure you'd enjoy it.
6 Why don't we make some placards? It's better than doing nothing.

a OK, I'll do it! They usually have food and music at those events, don't they?
b OK, I'll do it. Is that the sit-in at the theatre?
c I don't know. I've never been to a demonstration before!
d I don't know. I'm not sure we've got the right materials.
e OK, let's do it. What's everyone marching for?
f I don't know. The last time I did that, I only collected €10!

★ 2 🔊 **30** **Choose the correct options. Then listen and check.**

1 Let's go on a march tomorrow! Come *on* / *off*, it'll be fun.
2 How about starting a petition. I'm *think / sure* people will sign it!
3 Let's invent slogans! It's better *than / that* doing nothing!
4 A Why don't we make a banner?
   B I don't *think / know*. It's very windy outside.
5 A How about starting a collection?
   B OK, *I'm going to / I'll* do it.
6 A Do you want to be a volunteer?
   B *I'm not sure. / I don't think*. It's a bit difficult.

★★ 3 🔊 **31** **Complete the conversation with these words. Then listen and check.**

| I'll do that | it'll be fun | ~~I don't know~~ |
| I'm sure | it's better than | |

Alex Why don't we go to the demonstration today?
Bea   [1] *I don't know*. It's a bit cold out today.
Alex That doesn't matter! We can put warm clothes on.
Bea   Yes, but we haven't got a banner.
Alex [2] .... we can make one!
Bea   I don't know! I'm a bit tired.
Alex Come on. It's for a good cause and [3] ....
Bea   I guess [4] .... sitting on the sofa! OK, I'll do it. Let's get started on that banner.
Alex OK, [5] .... and you can make a placard.
Bea   OK, sounds great!

★★ 4 🔊 **31** **Listen to the conversation in Exercise 3 again. Are the sentences true (T) or false (F)?**

1 Everything is prepared for the demonstration. *F*
2 Bea isn't very sure about the idea. ....
3 Alex says they can buy a banner. ....
4 Alex persuades Bea to go to the demonstration. ....
5 Alex will make the placard. ....

★★ 5 **Write a conversation. Use phrases from Exercises 1–3 and this information:**

You're sitting with a friend. You want to join a protest march, but your friend wants to play a video game instead. Persuade your friend to go with you.

....
....
....
....
....
....
....

Speaking and Listening page 119

Grammar First conditional

★ **1** **Match the sentence beginnings (1–6) to the endings (a–f).**

1 If you help me,   *e*
2 If you want to stay out late,
3 If you make the banner,
4 We'll clean the kitchen,
5 We'll go on the march,
6 We'll prepare the party,

a if you think of some good slogans.
b if you send the invitations.
c if you cook lunch.
d I'll do the placards.
e I'll help you.
f you'll need to tidy your room first.

★ **2** **The Romeo protests. Put the words in the correct order.**

1 What will happen if / us / to / don't / they / listen / ?
   What will happen if they don't listen to us?
2 What will happen if / the / stops / the / mayor / demonstration / ?
   ....
3 If she doesn't appear, / will / march / to / a / organise / we / have
   ....
4 If she doesn't appear, / slogan / better / a / have / invent / we / to / will
   ....
5 If she doesn't appear, / need / sign / more / we / to / petition / will / people / the
   ....

★★ **3** **Write sentence endings. Use the correct form of the verbs.**

1 If I do well in these exams, I / get into / the school of my choice.
   If I do well in these exams, I'll get into the school of my choice.

2 If you access the webpage, you / get / lots of good ideas.
   ....

3 If I don't get home in time, I / miss / my favourite series on TV.
   ....

4 Her mum will be worried if / she / not arrive / home on time.
   ....

5 His father won't be happy if / anything happen / to the car.
   ....

6 Your pet will get ill if / you / not feed / it properly.
   ....

★★ **4** **Complete the replies with the correct form of the verbs.**

1 A What are you worried about?
   B If I *don't find* (not find) the house keys, I*'ll be* (be) in trouble!
2 A Will you wash the car?
   B If I .... (wash) the car, ... (you/give) me some money?
3 A Where are my glasses?
   B If you .... (look for) them, you .... (find) them!
4 A What's the capital of Mongolia?
   B .... (you/make) me some coffee if I .... (tell) you the answer?
5 A We're meeting at the café at 7.30.
   B .... (you/wait for) me if I .... (be) late?
6 A Sheena's invited you to her party.
   B What .... (happen) if I .... (not go) ?

Grammar Reference pages 98–99

Reading

1 Read the text quickly and choose the best headline.

   a Teenager gets a job in a magazine

   b Teenage protest produces results

   c Teenagers support digital photos

Who said teenagers don't care about the world around them? Who said that the only thing they worry about is chatting on social networks? Who said that protests never get anywhere? Here's a story to prove those people wrong!

In May 2012, a 13-year-old American girl went to the offices of a well-known teenage magazine to hand in a petition. She went there together with her mother and a group of girls who agree with her ideas. What were they protesting against? They said that too many magazine photos show 'fake' girls and women. They asked the magazine to be careful with how they use computer programmes to change a woman's image. They said that girls need to see 'something realistic' when they read their favourite magazines. Julia Bluhm, the 13-year-old, went into the magazine's offices and talked to one of the editors. As a result of that conversation, the magazine has promised to monitor how they process digital photos.

As you can see, protests can achieve results! If you feel strongly about a particular problem, you can talk to your friends and share your opinions. You can make up a petition and collect signatures. People will probably listen to you if you present them with reasonable arguments. They might not make *all* the changes you would like, but *something* will happen! So remember, like a famous president once said: 'Can we change? – Yes, we can!'

2 Read the text again and choose the correct options.

   1 People often say that teenagers *are /(aren't)* interested in current events.

   2 Julia Bluhm produced a *petition / slogan* for women.

   3 Julia and her friends protested against *all / some* digital photos.

   4 They think that magazine photos of women *are / aren't* realistic enough.

   5 The article concludes that change *is / isn't* possible.

Listening

1 🔊 32   Listen to the conversation. Choose the correct options.

   1 The *boy /(girl)* is keen on joining the march.

   2 The *boy / girl* had a friend who went to hospital.

   3 The *boy / girl* doesn't worry about the weather.

   4 The *boy / girl* worries about possible foot pain.

   5 The boy decides to go on the march because of the *food / good weather.*

2 🔊 32   Who says these phrases? Write B for boy or G for girl. Listen again and check.

   1 I can borrow   *G*

   2 we'll get wet   ....

   3 these things happen   ....

   4 I'll probably have to make a new one.   ....

   5 Didn't I tell you   ....

   6 All right, you win!   ....

Writing A formal letter

1 **Match the letter sections (1–3) to the examples (a–f).**

1 Opening
2 Reason for writing
3 Closing

a Kind regards   *3*
b Dear Mr Jones
c I am writing to comment on …
d Best wishes
e Dear *Teenmag*
f I am writing because …

2 **Complete the letter with these phrases.**

It is true	like my grandmother	So you see
~~The writer says~~	What can we do	

STAR LETTER

Dear *Teenmag*,

I am writing because I have just read an article in your magazine about old people living alone. ¹ *The writer says* that old people should all live together in special homes. I cannot agree with this idea. ² .... that some old people do not have any family to look after them, but many of them have. My grandmother lives alone and is very proud of this.

³ .... to help old people who prefer to live in their own homes? Perhaps we could organise volunteer groups to visit them. If they have company, they will feel better. If we help them, they can teach us a lot too, ⁴ .... I learn many things from her that I don't learn at school!

⁵ .... , it shouldn't be necessary to take old people out of their homes if they prefer to stay there.

Best wishes,
John Noonan

3 **Complete column A with information from John's letter.**

	A John letter	B My letter
Reason for writing	*doesn't agree with article*	
The problem		
A possible solution		

4 **You recently read an article about pets abandoned in the street. The article said that the animals should be captured and kept in cages at a special shelter. You don't agree with this idea. Write your main ideas in column B.**

5 **Write a formal letter to express your opinion. Use your ideas and the information and expressions from Exercises 1–4.**

....

....
....
....
....
....
....
....

....
....
....
....
....
....

....
....

Vocabulary Extreme adjectives

★ **1**   **Complete the sentences with these words.**

awful	boiling	brilliant
furious	huge	terrifying

1 The film wasn't just bad – it was *awful*!
2 The bull we saw wasn't just big – it was
.... !
3 The other driver wasn't just angry – he was
.... !
4 Walking through the tunnel in total darkness
wasn't just scary – it was .... !
5 When we got off the plane in Seville, it wasn't
just hot – it was .... !
6 Have you read this? It isn't just good – it's
.... !

Brain Trainer

Arrange these adjectives in order of size:

big   tiny   huge   small

Now do Exercise 2.

★ **2**   **Replace the <u>underlined</u> words with these adjectives.**

exhausted	freezing	furious
huge	thrilled	tiny

1 I wasn't wearing enough clothes for such a
<u>very cold</u> wind.   *freezing*
2 We met Beyoncé in a shop in London, and I
was <u>really excited</u>.   ....
3 At the zoo, I saw a baby kangaroo, and it was
<u>very, very small</u>.   ....
4 After six hours shopping in the sales, we felt
<u>extremely tired</u>.   ....
5 A truck crashed into a shop and made a <u>really
big</u> hole in the wall.   ....
6 My parents were <u>really angry</u> when they
saw the phone bill.   ....

Vocabulary page 111

★★ **3**   **Put the letters in the correct order to complete the text.**

Last winter we did a mountain trek of about
20 kilometres. We walked for hours through the
¹ *freezing* (greenfiz) snow, until we reached the top
of this mountain. The views from the top were
² .... (labtirlin): the people and cars
in the distance were just ³ .... (yint)
figures. Then my uncle took us to a special
area, where we climbed up into a
⁴ .... (eguh) tree. We had to wait half
an hour, but then we saw some wild animals
come to drink in the small lake. We were just
⁵ .... (helldirt) because they were so
close! And by the time we got back to the car, we
were all ⁶ .... (steedhaux).

★★ **4**   **Complete the conversation with these words.**

awful	boiling	brilliant	freezing	huge	tiny

A Did you have a good holiday?
B Yeah, in the end!
A What happened?
B My dad found an apartment building on the
internet that was really cheap. I mean, the
building was ¹ *huge*: it had 15 floors! But when
we got there, we discovered that the
apartment itself was ² .... for the
five of us. It only had two bedrooms and one
bathroom!
A Oh dear!
B And that's not all! The weather outside was
about 40 degrees – absolutely
³ .... But the air-conditioning
inside was really ⁴ .... I was so
cold I couldn't sleep well!
A So wasn't there anything good about the place?
B Well, the swimming pool was ⁵ .... :
it wasn't clean enough and there were too
many people. But we were still lucky, because
the beach was wonderful and the nightlife
was ⁶ .... ! There were lots of
good shops, cafés and discos so in the end
we didn't really spend much time in the
apartment.

Reading

★ **1** **Read the article quickly and answer the question.**

Which person has experience of saving someone? ....

Last week we had an article on risks that people take. This week we asked you the question:

Would you risk your life to save another person or an animal?

Here are some of your replies!

Eileen

I don't know! It's difficult to say, because I've never been in such an awful situation. I suppose if a child or a small animal was in trouble, I'd try to help. But I can't imagine that I would risk my life. I mean, I wouldn't jump into a freezing river, because I'm not very strong anyway. And I wouldn't run into a huge burning building either, because that's just too dangerous.

Brad

I'm a bit impulsive, so I might do something without thinking too much about it. Last summer at the beach for example, a little boy fell off a rock, and I was able to rescue him. I was exhausted afterwards, but also thrilled. If anything happened to my family or my close friends, I'd probably try to help immediately. But I wouldn't react the same with animals – I'm not an animal person!

Lenny

I don't think I'd risk my life, but in a terrifying situation you never know how you'll react. I don't think I'd take any unnecessary risks, but certainly if I thought I could help, I would do so.

★ **2** **Choose the correct options.**

1 Eileen _would_ / _wouldn't_ try to help a child or small animal.

2 She _would_ / _wouldn't_ take any serious risks.

3 Brad _often_ / _rarely_ does things without thinking about them.

4 He _is_ / _isn't_ keen on animals.

5 Lenny _is_ / _isn't_ sure about how he would react.

★★ **3** **Are the sentences true (T) or false (F)?**

1 Eileen has no experience of risking her life.   _T_

2 She's quite sure she's strong enough.   ....

3 Brad knows that he would act fast.   ....

4 Brad would help both people and animals.   ....

5 Lenny would probably try to help if it wasn't too risky.   ....

Grammar Second conditional

★ **1 Match the questions (1–6) to the answers (a–f).**

1 If you had the chance, would you ski down a mountain? *c*
2 If there was an awful fire in the building, would you know what to do?
3 Would you jump into the water if your pet fell into a river?
4 What would you do if you had enough money?
5 Where would you go if you wanted a brilliant adventure holiday?
6 If you had to choose only one friend, who would it be?

a I don't think I would because I can't swim very well.
b No, I wouldn't. I'd just run for my life.
c I'd love to try, but I don't think I'm brave enough!
d I don't know! I wouldn't know who to choose.
e I think I'd buy a huge hotel for me and my family and friends!
f I'd probably go on safari in Africa.

★ **2 Match the sentence beginnings (1–6) to the endings (a–f).**

1 If someone gave me a bicycle, *b*
2 If I had to stay in the jungle,
3 If my family had an apartment at the beach,
4 We'd have a bigger dog
5 We'd go swimming in the lake
6 I'd learn to ride a horse

a I'd go there every weekend!
b I'd use it to go to school.
c I think I'd worry about the snakes.
d if it wasn't so expensive.
e if we had room in our flat.
f if it was allowed.

★★ **3 Put the words in the correct order to make the questions.**

1 What would happen / if / father's / I / keys / my / car / hid / ?
What would happen if I hid my father's car keys?
2 What would I do / school / if / to / I / go / didn't / today / ?
....
3 If I didn't go to school, / get / would / trouble / I / into / ?
....
4 If I didn't live in my neighbourhood, / live / where / would / I / ?
....
5 If I didn't live in my neighbourhood, / about / I / what / miss / would / it / ?
....
6 What would I buy / if / lots of / I / had / money / ?
....

★★ **4 Write sentences. Use the Second conditional.**

1 If I wasn't so tired, I / stay / watch the film.
If I wasn't so tired, I'd stay to watch the film.
2 If this book was more interesting, I / finish / reading it.
....
3 If the weather wasn't freezing, we / go / for a long walk.
....
4 I'd help you with your homework, if / I / have / more time.
....
5 We'd stay longer, if we / not have to / catch the last bus.
....
6 They'd be much happier, if / it / not rain / so much.
....

★★ **5 Complete the answers with the correct form of the verbs.**

1 A Don't you know the answer?
   B If I *knew* (know) the answer, I *wouldn't ask* (not ask) you!
2 A Do you like the jacket?
   B Oh, yes! If I .... (have) the money, I ....
   (buy) it!
3 A What's the matter?
   B If I .... (have) a map, I .... (not be) lost!
4 A Where did you hear that joke?
   B You .... (not believe) me if I .... (tell) you!
5 A Do you like my new shoes?
   B I .... (not wear) them, even if you ....
   (pay) me to!
6 A Should I tell him the truth?
   B He .... (be) very disappointed if you
   .... (lie) to him.

Grammar Reference pages 100–101

Vocabulary Illness and injury

★ **1** Read the clues and complete the puzzle. What's the eleventh word?

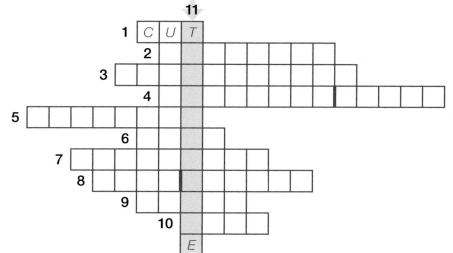

11

| 1 | C | U | T |

Clues:
1 You might get this on your finger if you have an accident with a knife.
2 When your head hurts.
3 This usually happens after you've eaten too much.
4 You might get this after a bad fall. It would make it painful to walk.
5 My dad got this when he was moving heavy furniture.
6 You can get this from fire or from the sun!
7 This is a problem for the dentist.
8 This often happens after shouting too much at a football match.
9 This is the noise you make when you force air through your throat.
10 You often get this on your skin if you have an allergy.
11 You have this when your body feels too hot.

★ **2** Complete the doctor's sentences with these words.

a cold	a cough	a rash
a sprained ankle	a temperature	backache

1 I was walking along the street when I put my foot in a hole and I fell down.
   You've got *a sprained ankle*.
2 My brother was putting the big suitcase in the car when he had this pain.
   He's got ....
3 I woke up during the night and I couldn't stop making this noise.
   You've got ....
4 My nose is bad, I use tissues all the time, I can't speak clearly.
   You've got ....
5 My legs are covered with little red marks!
   You've got ....
6 I'm too hot, I don't feel well, I'm really thirsty.
   You've got ....

★★ **3** Match the problems (1–6) to the suggestions (a–f).

1 a burn   *e*
2 a cut
3 a headache
4 a sore throat
5 a stomachache
6 toothache

a Why don't you take some of this medicine?
b You should go to the dentist!
c Don't eat or drink anything until you feel better.
d You should cover that with a bandage.
e Put lots of cold water on it.
f How about some aspirin?

★★ **4** Put the letters in the correct order to complete the teacher's report.

Most of the children this winter have had the usual ¹*coughs* (hugsoc) and ² .... (dolcs). Three of them have appeared in class with a ³ .... (arumperette), so I had to send them home. Many of them also complained of ⁴ .... (shadecahe), probably because of the heating in the school. One boy appeared with a ⁵ .... (nurb) on his hand, obviously from playing with matches. But nobody has had any ⁶ .... (shears), unlike last year, when we had a lot.

What's the matter?

Vocabulary page 111

 **Talking about health**

Speaking and Listening

★ 1 🔊 33 **Choose the correct options. Then listen and check.**

1 What's the *ache / matter*?
2 I've got a sprained *nose / ankle*.
3 *Are / Do* you all right?
4 How *do / does* it feel?
5 Not too *good / better*.
6 How *do / does* you feel?
7 A bit *better / worse*, thanks.

★ 2 🔊 34 **Put the sentences in the correct order. Then listen and check.**

a What's the matter, Monica? ...1.
b It means you won't be able to walk for at least a week. ....
c You've got a sprained ankle. ....
d Does this hurt? ....
e Oww! Yes, it does. ....
f What does that mean? ....
g Oh, no! ....
h I was hiking in the countryside when I fell over a stone. ....

★★ 3 🔊 35 **Complete the conversation with these phrases. Then listen and check.**

a bit better now	do you feel	does it feel
~~I burned myself~~	That's awful	the matter

Betsy That looks painful! What happened to you?
Bob ¹*I burned myself* in the kitchen.
Betsy What were you doing?
Bob I was helping to cook lunch. Fried fish.
Betsy So?
Bob The fish slipped out of my fingers and I got burning hot oil all over my hand.
Betsy ²......................! What did you do?
Bob My mum turned the tap on, and I held my hand under the running water. Then we got a cloth with some ice in it, and came straight here to see the doctor.
Betsy How ³......................?
Bob It's still a bit painful. But what about you? What's ⁴...................... with your hand?
Betsy I was cutting up vegetables, and the knife slipped.
Bob How ⁵......................?
Betsy Well, I got a bit scared because I don't like seeing blood. But I'm feeling ⁶......................, thanks.
Bob That's good. I hate seeing blood, too.

★★ 4 🔊 35 **Listen to the conversation in Exercise 3 again. Tick (✓) the correct box.**

	Bob	Betsy	Both
1 accident in the kitchen			✓
2 hot oil			
3 kitchen knife			
4 used cold water			
5 went to the doctor's			

★★ 5 **Write a conversation. Use phrases from Exercises 1–3 and this information:**

You go to visit a friend, and you find him/her ill in bed. Talk about his/her health. Explain something similar which happened to you last year.

Speaking and Listening page 120

Grammar Relative pronouns

⭐ **1** **Match the sentence beginnings (1–6) to the endings (a–f).**

1 That's the stadium   *e*
2 That's the singer
3 There's the shop
4 This is the pump
5 She's the journalist
6 That's the wall

a who wrote the article.
b which I use for my bike.
c which I fell off.
d where I bought my bike.
e where our team won the championship.
f who gave me an autograph.

⭐ **2** **Choose the correct options.**

1 These are the photos *where / which* we took on holiday.
2 This is the guide *which / who* showed us round the city.
3 This is the restaurant *where / which* we had my birthday dinner.
4 These are some Irish students *which / who* we met in the park.
5 This is the entrance to the theme park *where / which* I told you about.
6 Here's the river *where / which* we took a boat trip.

⭐ **3** **Complete the conversation with *who*, *which*, or *where*.**

A Who are the people in this picture?
B They're the ones ¹ *who* went on a skiing trip to the Alps.
A What happened to that boy on the left?
B He's the one ² .... got a sprained ankle on the first day!
A What a shame! And what's that in the girl's hand?
B That's the helmet ³ .... she wore to protect her head.
A And in the background?
B That's the park ⁴ .... we had a picnic lunch.
A What's that black thing there?
B That's the place ⁵ .... we made a small fire to keep warm!
A Very nice! And are those your skis?
B No, they're the ones ⁶ .... I borrowed from another student. They were much better than mine!

⭐⭐ **4** **Make sentences with *who*, *which* or *where*.**

1 This is the dog / bite me / when / we be / on holiday.
   This is the dog which bit me when we were on holiday.
2 This is the park / everything happen.
   ....
3 Here's the car / my father / take me / to the hospital / in.
   ....
4 This is the doctor / look at / my leg.
   ....
5 That's the needle / he use / to give me an injection.
   ....
6 This is the nurse / put a bandage / on the bite.
   ....
7 Here's the room / I have to wait / afterwards.
   ....

Grammar Reference pages 100–101

Reading

1 Read the questions and choose the best answer.

2 Read the score box and check your answers.

Listening

1 🔊 36 **Listen and answer the questions.**

1 There are .... people in the conversation.
  a 2 **b** 3 **c** 4

2 They're talking .... .
  a in the hospital
  b at home
  c at the doctor's

3 The boy had a .... accident.
  a walking
  b bicycle
  c car

4 He has problems with his .... .
  a knee and legs
  b eyes and neck
  c stomach and back

5 The doctor checked the injuries .... .
  a immediately
  b after an hour
  c after two hours

2 🔊 36 **Who says these phrases? Write M for mother, S for son or U for uncle. Listen again and check.**

1 I'm much better   *S*
2 an awful accident   ....
3 sprained his knee   ....
4 How did it feel?   ....
5 Not too good!   ....
6 How did it happen?   ....

Would you know how to survive in an extreme environment?

Do our questionnaire and find out!

1 If you got lost in the jungle, what would you do?
  a make a fire with lots of smoke
  b find a river and follow it downstream
  c climb a big tree to check your location

2 If you were exhausted after walking in deep snow and it got dark, what would you do?
  a dig a hole in the snow and sleep inside it
  b lie down behind a big rock and sleep
  c try to stay awake and keep walking

3 If you were up a mountain and a terrifying storm began, what would you do?
  a get down off the mountain as quickly as possible
  b keep walking until you found a cave
  c sit under a big tree until the storm passed

4 If you were walking in the countryside and met a huge bull, what would you do?
  a walk backwards slowly and carefully
  b stand completely still and wait for the bull to go away
  c turn round and run away

5 If you sprained your ankle in the mountains, what would you do?
  a try and find an area with coverage for your mobile phone
  b use a mirror to make SOS signals in the sun
  c make a fire with lots of smoke

Writing An application form

1 Match the question words (1–6) to the answers (a–f).

1 Who   *f*
2 What
3 Where
4 When
5 Why
6 How many

a because that's our timetable!
b twenty-five
c school assembly
d in the main hall
e at 8.30 in the morning
f my class

2 Make questions for the <u>underlined</u> words.

1 There are <u>five</u> people in my family.
   How many people are there in your family?
2 We live <u>in a flat near a park</u>.
   ....
3 <u>No</u>, I've <u>never been abroad</u>.
   ....
4 I'd like to go <u>because I think it would be very interesting</u>.
   ....
5 I play sports <u>three times a week</u>.
   ....
6 I'll be <u>15</u> next April.
   ....
7 I usually go to concerts with <u>three of my friends</u>.
   ....

3 Read the application form. Are the sentences true (T) or false (F)?

1 Mervyn can't run very fast.   *T*
2 He's had several pets.   ....
3 He probably likes taking risks.   ....
4 He's not keen on rhinos.   ....
5 He probably wouldn't know what to do in an emergency in the park.   ....

4 Now complete the application form yourself.

LITTLE AFRICA SAFARI PARK ▌▌▌▌▌▌▌▌▌▌▌

Application form

Name: *Mervyn Williams*   Age: *15*

1 How many of these things can you do? Tick the boxes.
   swim ☑   run fast ☐   climb trees ☑
   use a canoe ☐   take underwater photos ☐

2 How many of these things have you done? Tick the boxes. Say when you did them.
   look after a pet ☐   ....
   visit the zoo ☑   *I went last year with the school.*
   work with animals ☐   ....
   go abroad ☑   *I went to France in 2009.*

3 What kind of person do people say you are? Circle three words.
   (quiet)   noisy   shy   (adventurous)   thoughtful   impulsive   patient   (impatient)

4 Which kind of animal would you prefer NOT to see? Tick the boxes. Say why.
   camels ☐   crocodiles ☐   hyenas ☑   lions ☐   rhinos ☐   snakes ☑
   Hyenas are really ugly and I'm afraid of snakes.

5 Write three things you would like to do in the safari park.
   1 *ride on a camel*
   2 *see a crocodile*
   3 *take photos*

6 Have you read the safety instructions in the visitors' guide?   Yes ☐   No ☑

LITTLE AFRICA SAFARI PARK ▌▌▌▌▌▌▌▌▌▌▌

Application form

Name: ....   Age: ....

1 How many of these things can you do? Tick the boxes.
   swim ☐   run fast ☐   climb trees ☐
   use a canoe ☐   take underwater photos ☐

2 How many of these things have you done? Tick the boxes. Say when you did them.
   look after a pet ☐   ....
   visit the zoo ☐   ....
   work with animals ☐   ....
   go abroad ☐   ....

3 What kind of person do people say you are? Circle three words.
   quiet   noisy   shy   adventurous   thoughtful   impulsive   patient   impatient

4 Which kind of animal would you prefer NOT to see? Tick the boxes. Say why.
   camels ☐   crocodiles ☐   hyenas ☐   lions ☐   rhinos ☐   snakes ☐
   ....

5 Write three things you would like to do in the safari park.
   1 ....
   2 ....
   3 ....

6 Have you read the safety instructions in the visitors' guide?   Yes ☐   No ☐

9 Inventions

Vocabulary Machine nouns and verbs

★ **1** Match the sentence beginnings (1–6) to the endings (a–f).

1 This product will run on a battery   *e*
2 To switch on the machine,
3 Then use the keyboard
4 To attach files to an email,
5 If you want to watch TV,
6 Don't forget to switch off

a press the round button in the corner.
b click on the 'Attach' button at the bottom.
c the machine when you've finished.
d you can also use the remote control.
e or you can plug the cable into a socket.
f to type in your password.

★★ **2** Put the letters in the correct order to complete the sentences.

1 Has anyone seen the *remote control* (meteor clorton)? I need it to change channels!
2 You can't play a car racing game without a .... (hewel) to move the car!
3 Oh no! The .... (trytabe) has died in the middle of the game!
4 It probably goes faster if you use the .... (beardyok) controls.
5 You can't watch this without an HDMI .... (belac).
6 If you press that .... (tontub), you'll delete all your work!
7 Take the cable out of the .... (costek) before you go to bed!
8 This is a special plastic .... (beut) to keep all the electric cables in.

★ **3** Complete the conversation with these words.

button	cable	plugged it in	press
~~remote control~~	socket	switched it on	

A What are you doing?
B We're trying to watch a film, but we can't open the file.
A Have you selected the file with the ¹*remote control*?
B Yes, that's it there.
A Have you checked the ² .... ?
B Which one?
A The one that goes from the computer to the TV.
B Yes, John ³ ....
A Yes, but is it in the right ⁴ .... ?
B I don't know!
A OK, I've changed it. Now ⁵ .... the 'Enter' ⁶ ....
B Hey! It's open! But I can't hear anything!
A You need to check the volume control then. Have you ⁷ .... ?
B Yes, that's it now. Thanks!

★★ **4** Complete the text with the correct form of these verbs.

attach	~~communicate~~	invent
plug in	press	switch off

How do you ¹*communicate* with your friends? Sending emails was OK, until someone ² .... text messages on mobile phones. Now mobile phones do the same things as a computer, and they're much more convenient (unless you forget to ³ .... the battery to recharge!). Touch screens are amazing: you don't even have to ⁴ .... buttons anymore! Nowadays I use a special application that works with Wi-Fi. I can chat with my friends, and it's very cheap. But it can be expensive if you forget to ⁵ .... the internet access or if you ⁶ .... a lot of photos or videos to a message.

Vocabulary page 112

Reading

⭐ **1** Read the text and put the paragraphs in the correct order.

1 _C._ 2 .... 3 .... 4 .... 5 ....

A In the second stage, the drawings are computerised by the keyboard programmers. This is when the characters start to move. Then all the colours are attached, so the places and movements look real. These are like the building blocks for the whole game.

B The final stage is just as important as the other ones: game testing. A selection of players are asked to use the game and communicate any operating problems they find. Once these problems are solved, the game is ready for you to switch on and play!

C Most of us have shared an afternoon playing video games with friends, but how many of us know how the games are made? Let me tell you about the process in four basic stages.

D In the third stage, the parts of the story are put in order. Next, the player options are produced. This is done by specialised programmers. So now the game has its two key parts: the different levels of difficulty and all the tasks for the players.

E First of all, you should know that most games are produced by a team who work closely together. They have lots of meetings where the basic story and characters are discussed. Once these components are agreed on, artists produce a set of drawings. The drawings illustrate the characters and the places in the game. For example, an old castle, a sports stadium or a futuristic city.

⭐ **2** Who does what? Match the actions (1–5) to the people (a–e).

1 invent the story and characters _d_
2 make the first drawings
3 computerise the drawings
4 create the options for players
5 check the game for problems

a a group of players
b keyboard programmers
c specialised programmers
d the team
e artists

⭐⭐ **3** Are the sentences true (T) or false (F)?

1 One person is responsible for the story. _F_
2 The characters' movements are built in the second stage. ....
3 Programmers do their jobs in the second and third stages. ....
4 Most video games have three main parts. ....
5 The testing stage is the most important one. ....
6 Most games are developed in four different stages. ....

Grammar Present simple passive

★ **1** Choose the correct options.

Radio-controlled cars ¹*is* / *are* operated by a remote control. Two sets of batteries ²*is* / *are* needed for the toy to function correctly. A large battery ³*is* / *are* located in the body of the car, and a smaller battery ⁴*is* / *are* placed in the remote control. A radio signal ⁵*is* / *are* sent from the remote control to the car. The speed and direction of the car ⁶*is* / *are* controlled by the buttons you press on the remote control.

★★ **2** Match the sentence beginnings (1–6) to the endings (a–f).

1 First the cars are   *e*
2 Next the design is
3 Then the parts are
4 Next they are
5 Then everything is
6 Finally the new cars are

a checked by computer.
b transported to the showrooms.
c produced in a factory.
d assembled in another factory.
e designed in the laboratory.
f created by the engineers.

★★ **3** Complete the questions, then add the correct answers.

1 *Are* cars made in Korea?
Yes, *they are.*
2 .... olive oil produced in England?
No, ...
3 .... mobile phones repaired here?
No, ...
4 .... phone batteries sold separately?
Yes, sometimes ....
5 .... rice grown in Spain?
Yes, ...
6 .... batteries provided with all your products?
No, ...
7 .... these TVs equipped with the necessary cables?
Yes, some of them ....

★★ **4** Make questions.

1 A Where / the best cars / produce?
Where are the best cars produced?
B In Germany!
2 A these oranges / grow / locally?
....
B No, they aren't.
3 A How / this program / install / on the computer?
....
B By following the instructions on the screen!
4 A Why / the cables / not provide / with the TVs?
....
B Because different people use different cables!
5 A Where / those watches / sell?
....
B Only in specialised shops.
6 A How / these lorries / build?
....
B I really don't know!

Vocabulary Word building

Active and passive

★ **5** **Rewrite the sentences in the passive. Include by + noun only if necessary.**

1 People in Italy design these clothes.

These clothes are designed in Italy.

2 Our chef prepares all our famous dishes.

....
....
....
....

3 Someone sells CDs like those in the street market.

....
....
....
....

4 We ask passengers not to stand near the doors.

....
....
....
....

5 The president of the club writes these articles.

....
....
....
....

6 People usually cook this kind of meat in a spicy sauce.

....
....
....
....

7 Shakira sings all the songs on this album.

....
....
....
....

★ **1** **Choose the correct options.**

1 Mobile phones have been a very popular *inventor / invention*.

2 Who was the *designer / design* of the first MP3 players?

3 We visited the capital and we loved the old *builders / buildings* there.

4 Cars and video games are some of Japan's most famous *producers / products*.

5 Monet is one of my favourite *painters / paintings*.

6 I'd love to know more about where *writers / writing* came from.

★ **2** **Look at the reading text on page 77. Find nouns for the verbs (1–5).**

1 move   *movements*
2 select   ....
3 play   ....
4 program   ....
5 draw   ....

★★ **3** **Complete the words with the correct ending.**

1 I think the computer is the most important invent*ion* of all time.
2 For me, Goya is the most original paint....... of all time.
3 My mum doesn't like these modern build....... she prefers old ones.
4 Our company sells only top-quality prod....... .
5 Armani is my sister's favourite fashion design....... .
6 What does this note say? I can't read the writ....... .

★★ **4** **Complete the conversations with the correct form of these words.**

build (x2)	~~design~~	invent	produce	write (x2)

1 A Why are these shoes so expensive?
   B Because they're *designed* by Manolo Blahnik!

2 A Who were the .... of the great cathedrals?
   B Nobody really knows their names!

3 A Why are these called personalised poems?
   B Because they're specially .... for individual people.

4 A What does a film .... do?
   B He or she finds the money to make the film.

5 A Who was the .... of TV?
   B A man called John Logie Baird.

6 A Are these houses strong?
   B I hope so! They're .... of concrete and brick.

7 A What kind of .... is this? I've never seen it before.
   B It looks like Chinese.

8 A What kind of .... are made here?
   B We make boots and shoes.

Grammar Reference pages 102–103

Vocabulary page 112

Chatroom — Problems with machines

Speaking and Listening

★ **1** 🔊 37 **Match the questions (1–5) to the answers (a–e). Then listen and check.**

1 What's the problem?   *b*
2 Have you checked the battery?
3 Have you checked the earphones?
4 There might be something wrong with the connection.
5 Have you checked that it's plugged in?

a No, I haven't, and it's not. How silly of me!
b My MP3 player doesn't work.
c OK, I'll check that first.
d They worked all right this morning.
e Yes, I bought a new one yesterday.

★ **2** 🔊 38 **Choose the correct options. Then listen and check.**

A You don't look very happy! What's the problem?
B The projector doesn't [1] *move /* (*work*).
A Are you sure? I used it at the weekend.
B Well, it's switched [2] *on / off*, but it's not showing the film.
A There might be something [3] *problem / wrong* with the cable.
B I don't think so. It's in the correct [4] *battery / socket*.
A Have you [5] *broken / checked* the F5 button?
B Oh, right! That's it! You're a genius!

★ **3** 🔊 39 **Complete the conversation with these phrases. Then listen and check.**

~~broken~~	checked them
I haven't tried that	pressed the button
see the images	something wrong

A What's the problem?
B My digital camera is [1] *broken*.
A Are you sure? You were taking photos yesterday.
B I know, but not any more.
A There might be [2] .... with the battery.
B I've checked that and it's OK.
A Have you [3] .... to switch it on?
B Yes! Look, the blue light's on.
A OK. What about the settings then? Have you [4] .... ?
B What settings?
A The symbols on the wheel.
B Ah, no, [5] ....
A Well, try turning it round, to check the different symbols.
B Wait a minute. Now I can see the image on the screen!
A Can I take a look? You had the wrong setting. That's why you couldn't [6] ....

★★ **4** 🔊 39 **Listen to the conversation in Exercise 3 again. Write the three things they checked.**

1 ....
2 ....
3 ....

★★ **5** **Write a conversation. Use phrases from Exercises 1–3 and this information:**

A friend is having problems with his/her video console. Ask them to explain the problem; make suggestions about how to solve the problem.

....
....
....
....
....

Speaking and Listening page 121

Grammar Past simple passive

★ 1 Complete the questions and answers.

1 *Was* the first smartphone produced in 1994?
Yes, *it was*.

2 .... more laptops than desktops sold in 2008?
Yes, ...

3 .... digital cameras invented in Japan?
No, ...

4 .... the first TV built in the USA?
No, ...

5 .... your CDs replaced by MP3s?
Yes, ...

★★ 2 Complete the sentences with the correct form of these verbs.

catch	fly	forget	grow
keep	sell	sing	~~write~~

1 This famous book was *written* by Tolkien.
2 These songs were .... only on special occasions.
3 Some scrolls were .... in libraries for hundreds of years.
4 Kites were .... for the first time in ancient China.
5 Thanks to the invention of books, old stories were not ....
6 Fish were .... here until the river became too polluted.
7 The palace was .... because the family needed the money.
8 Cotton was .... in ancient Egypt.

Brain Trainer

Notice what happens to the position of the main noun when a sentence is transformed from active to passive.

Active: Tolkein wrote *this book*.
Passive: *This book* was written by Tolkein

★★ 3 Make questions.

1 A cars / invent / in Germany?
Were cars invented in Germany?
B Probably, but I'm not sure.

2 A When / the Arctic Monkeys' first album / release?
....
B That was in 2006!

3 A When / Michael Jackson's last concert / hold?
....
B I think that was in 1997.

4 A Which famous English icon / kill / New York in 1980?
....
B It was John Lennon.

5 A What / Stephenie Meyer's first book / call?
....
B *Twilight*. It's the most famous one.

★★ 4 Rewrite the sentences in the passive. Include *by* + noun only if necessary.

1 The Americans elected Barack Obama as president in 2008.
Barack Obama was elected as president in 2008.

2 A tornado destroyed ten houses last week.
....
....

3 Police rescued three children from the sea on Monday.
....
....

4 Someone stole the school sports trophies last night!
....
....

5 A teacher saw three cats on the school roof this morning.
....
....

6 Ten thousand people signed the petition to keep the local library open.
....
....

Grammar Reference pages 102–103

Reading

1 Read the texts quickly and match the names (1–3) to their preferences (a–c).

1 Natalia		**a** cars
2 Ted		**b** electric guitars
3 Chris		**c** internet

>>>

Last week we asked you to tell us about your favourite inventions. Here is a selection of your replies.

Natalia

For me, the greatest invention ever is the car! Life wouldn't be the same without cars. Obviously, I don't drive yet, but I help my dad with our car. We watch Formula 1 races on TV, and sometimes we go to see the real thing if there's a competition in our area. I get car magazines and read about the latest models. When I'm older, I'd really like to buy a smart German sports car.

My favourite invention is the internet! Laptops and smartphones are fun, but it's the internet that makes everything possible. I can use it for entertainment but also to study with. My parents do quite a lot of shopping on the internet, too. But above all I use it for social networking: I have to know where my friends are and what they're doing!

Ted

Chris

I'd say that electric guitars are my favourite invention. If we didn't have them, we wouldn't have any concerts and life would be dull! Concerts are really important for me, they've got such an atmosphere and you can feel the music, not like on CDs. But I also play the guitar and spend a lot of time practising with friends. I learn a lot from watching the guitarists on TV, too.

2 Are the sentences true (T) or false (F)?

1 Natalia only sees car races on TV. *F*

2 Ted uses the internet for three different reasons. ....

3 Chris thinks studio music is the best. ....

4 Natalia also plays a musical instrument. ....

5 Ted's main priority is contact with his friends. ....

6 Chris's main priority is music. ....

Listening

1 🔊 **40** Listen and complete the summary of the conversation. Use one word in each space.

Ally helps Ben, who has a problem with the [1] *video*. First they check the [2] .... cable, then the [3] .... cable and finally the [4] .... cable. Next, Ally realises there might be something wrong with the input source on the [5] .... In the end, she uses the [6] .... to solve the problem.

2 🔊 **40** Listen again and put these phrases in the order you hear them.

a in the wrong socket ....

b the hard disk drive ....

c the power cable ....

d Here you are. ....

e It's both, actually. *1*

Writing An opinion essay

1 Put the parts of an opinion essay in the correct order.

a Second, using an e-book, you don't have to carry so many heavy school books. ....

b In my opinion, e-books are a really important invention. ....

c In conclusion, our life would be much simpler if we used more e-books. ....

d First, because many different books can be stored in them. ....

e An important invention .1..

f Finally, e-books save huge amounts of paper and trees. ....

2 Complete the opinion essay with these words.

fast and safe	~~important inventions~~
my social life	that's not true
the other traffic	

An invention I couldn't live without.

In my opinion, there are many ¹*important inventions*, but I couldn't live without my mountain bike.

First, it's my normal means of transport. I use it to go to and from school every day. It's ² .... , it doesn't cost anything, and it doesn't pollute the town, not like ³ .... In fact, I have to be careful not to breathe all the fumes from the traffic!

Second, it's a great way to get exercise. Everyone talks about teenagers sitting on sofas playing video games and eating the wrong kind of food, but ⁴ .... for all of us!

Finally, it's an important part of ⁵ .... For example, at weekends I go out on excursions with friends and, if I didn't have my bike, I wouldn't know so many people!

In conclusion, my life wouldn't be the same without my bike.

3 You are going to write an essay with the same title. Complete the table with your ideas.

An invention I couldn't live without	
Paragraph 1: introduction	¹ ....
Paragraphs 2–4: reasons and example(s)	² .... ³ .... ⁴ ....
Paragraph 5: conclusion	⁵ ....

4 Now write an opinion essay. Use your ideas and information and expressions in Exercises 1 –3.

....
....
....
....
....
....
....
....
....
....
....
....
....
....

Grammar

1 **Choose the correct options.**

0 Tell me your plan! What .... do now?
a will you   **b** are you   **c** are you going to

1 Her mum says that Sue .... until she's finished tidying her room.
a won't leave
b isn't going to leave
c doesn't leave

2 I don't think I .... pizza – I'm bored with pizza!
a have   **b** won't have   **c** 'm going to have

3 They've already decided: they .... write to the newspaper.
a 'll   **b** are going to   **c** are

4 Here's the woman .... gave us the tickets for the concert!
a where   **b** which   **c** who

5 These are the presents .... we bought for the family.
a where   **b** which   **c** who

/ 5 marks

2 **Make sentences.**

0 If you don't help me with the housework, I / not / give you a lift in the car.
If you don't help me with the housework, I won't give you a lift in the car

1 She / take you shopping if you ask her nicely!
....
....

2 If I / know / how to repair the camera, I'd do it for you!
....
....

3 If you don't leave some money for the waiter, he / not be / very happy!
....
....

4 What would happen if / not rain / all year?
....
....

5 If you had to go to school on Saturdays, what / you do / on Sundays?
....
....

/ 5 marks

3 **Complete the text with the passive forms of the verbs.**

The world's first aeroplane took off in 1903, and began the race for better air machines. Many new kinds of planes ⁰*were developed* (develop) between the two world wars. Jets and helicopters ¹........................ (build) during the Second World War, and the first commercial jet flight ²........................ (operate) in the 1950s. Concorde, the world's fastest commercial planes, ³........................ (run) between 1969 and 2003. However, this kind of jet ⁴........................ (not produce) anymore. Nowadays, modern aeroplanes ⁵........................ (design) to use fuel more efficiently.

/ 5 marks

Vocabulary

4 **Complete the sentences with these words.**

agree with	argue with	believe in
~~care about~~	placards	slogans

0 I signed the petition because I *care about* my community.

1 We spent all morning making the .... for the demonstration.

2 We got together to write .... for our banners.

3 People join a march because they .... the reasons it was organised.

4 If we don't .... other people, there will never be any change.

5 I'm afraid I don't .... your ideas!

/ 5 marks

5 **Choose the correct options.**

0 A Why can't he walk very well?
   B He's got a *stomachache / toothache / sprained ankle*.

1 A Did you enjoy the film?
   B Yes. It was *awful / brilliant / boiling*!

2 A What have you done to your hand?
   B I've got a bad *cough / cold / rash*.

3 A Did you see the size of that pizza?
   B Big? It was absolutely *huge / freezing / thrilled*.

4 A I couldn't hear very well at the theatre.
  B Why not?
  A The woman behind me had a *headache / burn / cough*.

5 A Have you read this story?
  B No, and I'm not going to. I've heard it's *furious / terrifying / exhausted*.

/ 5 marks

6 Choose the correct options.

0 It won't work unless you turn this little .... here.
  a tube   **(b)** wheel   **c** keyboard

1 No wonder it doesn't work! It's not ....!
  a plugged in   **b** produced   **c** invented

2 Nowadays many people .... through chats and blogs.
  a attach   **b** build   **c** communicate

3 If you have problems with a computer cable, try checking the .... .
  a batteries   **b** sockets   **c** buttons

4 What was the name of the artist who produced this .... ?
  a paint   **b** painter   **c** painting

5 Historians have discovered the name of the original .... of the monument.
  a design   **b** designer   **c** designation

/ 5 marks

Speaking

7 Complete the conversation with one word in each gap.

A What's the problem?
B My mobile phone doesn't ⁰*work*. I can't make a call.
A Have you ¹........................ the battery?
B Yes, of course! Look!
A Have you tried ²........................ the message button?
B No, I haven't.
A Well, this message ³........................ you haven't got coverage! Anyway, what's the ⁴........................ with Ewan?
B He hasn't stopped all week.
A ⁵........................ does he feel?
B He says he feels absolutely exhausted – and he's got a ⁶........................ throat.
A Maybe he ⁷........................ lie down for a while. So, are you coming out for dinner?
B I don't know. What about Ewan?

A He'll be fine! ⁸........................ on, it's only an hour or two.
B I shouldn't leave him alone.
A Why not? It's ⁹........................ than staying at home.
B I'll tell you what. We'll get a takeaway and then we can eat here together.
A OK, you win! ¹⁰........................ do that.

/ 10 marks

Translation

8 Translate the sentences.

1 If we don't protest, no one will change anything!
....

2 What kind of slogan are you going to write?
....

3 The first car was invented by Karl Benz.
....

4 What would you do if you had a stomachache?
....

5 If I were you, I'd check the sockets on the laptop.
....

/ 5 marks

Dictation

9))) 41 **Listen and write.**

1 ....
2 ....
3 ....
4 ....
5 ....

/ 5 marks

Present simple and continuous

Present simple	Present continuous
He works in a café.	He's serving coffee at the moment.

Use

Present simple

We use the Present simple to talk about:

- routines and habits.
  We **get up** late at the weekend.
- things that are true in general.
  I **love** surprise parties!
  She **hates** news programmes on TV.

Time expressions

adverbs of frequency: *every day/week/year, on Fridays, at the weekend, in the morning, at night, after school*

Present continuous

We use the Present continuous to talk about:

- things that are happening at the moment of speaking.
  She**'s studying** in France at the moment.

Time expressions

now, right now, just now, at the moment, today, these days

Verb + -ing

Affirmative		
I/You/We/They	like watching	cartoons.
He/She/It	likes watching	

Negative		
I/You/We/They	don't like watching	cartoons.
He/She/It	doesn't like watching	

Questions
Do I/you/we/they like watching cartoons?
Does he/she/it like watching cartoons?

Use

We use *like, love, enjoy, don't mind, can't stand, hate* and *prefer* + verb + *-ing* to talk about things we like or don't like doing.

Form

The verbs *like, love, enjoy, don't mind, can't stand, hate* and *prefer* are followed by a verb ending in *-ing*.
I **don't mind watching** football on TV.

Spelling rules

most verbs: add *-ing*   *play → playing*
verbs that end with *-e*: drop the *-e* and add *-ing*   *come → coming*
verbs that end in one vowel + one consonant: double the consonant and add *-ing*   *sit → sitting*

Grammar practice

Present simple and continuous

1   Match the sentence beginnings (1–5) to the endings (a–e).

1 Bill drives a taxi   *c*
2 My grandparents love sweet things
3 Gerry travels a lot
4 My daughter plays the cello
5 Susan enjoys football

a and today he's flying to Russia.
b and she's watching a match right now.
c and now he's waiting for a passenger.
d and she's playing in a concert right now.
e and today they're having ice cream for dessert.

2   Complete the conversation with the Present simple or Present continuous form of the verbs.

A Welcome to summer camp! There are six beds in this room!
B I (want) [1] *want* one next to the window!
C And I (need) [2] .... one near the door!
D Tina! What (you/do) [3] .... ?
B I (put) [4] .... my things on this bed and the one next to it.
D Why?
B Because Becky (talk) [5] .... to the instructor now, and I (keep) [6] .... this bed for her.
D OK, but you (have got) [7] .... an extra pillow on your bed and I (not have got) [8] .... any. Can you give it to me?
B Sure! Here you are!

3 Write sentences.

1 A What / do / Tuesdays?
What do you do on Tuesdays?
B I / usually / go / the library.
....

A What / do / today?
....
B Today / I / study / for an exam.
....

2 A Where / Amy / live?
....
B Her family / have / house / on the coast.
.... ,
but she / live / here with her aunt /
at the moment.
....

3 A What / John / do / right now?
....
B He / wait / for the bus.
....
A What time / it / leave?
....
B I / not / sure. Maybe / it's / late.
....

Verb + -ing

4 Complete the text with the correct form of these verbs.

hang	have	listen	live
~~look~~	take	wait	watch

We live in a flat on the tenth floor! I like ¹ *looking* out of the window at all the people down in the street, and I love ² .... to the rain on the walls when there's a storm. We can see the station too, and my grandfather enjoys ³ .... all the trains come and go. But there are some things I don't like very much. I don't mind ⁴ .... the dog out for a walk because I love the fresh air, but I hate ⁵ .... to take the rubbish out to the bins. I prefer ⁶ .... until someone else goes down, then my brother or my parents take it out. And I can't stand ⁷ .... the clothes on the balcony because sometimes the wind blows them away. I love ⁸ .... so high up, because I don't feel so small anymore.

5 Put the words in the correct order.

1 doesn't / morning / mind / his / He / bed / in / making / the
He doesn't mind making his bed in the morning.

2 coffee / mother / enjoys / on / My / the / having / patio
....
....

3 attic / Peter / alone / hates / in / being / the / !
....
....

4 front / like / sitting / bus / at / doesn't / the / of / She / the
....
....

5 loves / fireplace / watching / the / in / Katy / the / flames
....
....

6 stand / I / to / can't / smoking / next / people / me
....
....

7 across / The / running / dogs / lawn / love / the
....
....

8 blinds / Pat / with / the / sleeping / closed / prefers
....
....

Past simple

Regular verbs: affirmative and negative

I/You/He/She/It/We/They	lived	in an old house.
I/You/He/She/It/We/They	didn't (did not) live	in an old house.

Irregular verbs: affirmative and negative

I/You/He/She/It/We/They	went	to London.
I/You/He/She/It/We/They	didn't (did not) go	to London.

Regular verbs: questions and short answers

Did I/you/he/she/it/we/they graduate from university?
Yes, I/you/he/she/it/we/they did.
No, I/you/he/she/it/we/they didn't (did not).

Irregular verbs: questions and short answers

Did I/you/he/she/it/we/they see a ghost?
Yes, I/you/he/she/it/we/they did.
No, I/you/he/she/it/we/they didn't (did not).

Wh- questions

What did he do?   Where did they go?

Use

We use the Past simple to talk about:

- finished actions in the past.
  *I **went** to the beach last weekend.*

Time expressions

adverbials of past time: *last night/week/month/year, an hour/week/year ago, in 2001, in the 20th century*

Past continuous

Affirmative

I/He/She/It	was talking	in class.
You/We/They	were talking	

Negative

I/He/She/It	wasn't (was not) talking	in class.
You/We/They	weren't (were not) talking	

Questions and short answers

Was I/he/she/it talking in class?	Yes, I/he/she/it was. No, I/he/she/it wasn't.
Were you/we/they talking in class?	Yes, you/we/they were. No, you/we/they weren't.

Wh- questions

What were they doing in the library yesterday?

Use

We use the Past continuous to talk about:

- an action in progress in the past.
  *Sean and I **were talking** about you last night!*

Time expressions

often used with particular points in past time:
yesterday morning, at 7 o'clock last Sunday, in the summer of 2012

Past simple vs Past continuous

long action	short action
We were taking a photo	when a man walked in front of the camera.

short action	long action
A man walked in front of the camera	while we were taking a photo.

Use

We often use both tenses together in order to distinguish between different actions.

- Past continuous for a longer action in progress.
- Past simple for a shorter action interrupting the other.
- *while* introduces a longer action.
- *when* introduces a shorter action.

Grammar practice

Past simple

1 Make sentences with the Past simple.

1 My aunt / show / us / lovely photos /
of her childhood.
*My aunt showed us lovely photos of her
childhood.*

2 Our cousins / take / lots of / silly pictures /
on / their school trip.
....

3 Their photos / be / blurred.
....

4 The album / be / full of / old-fashioned photos.
....

5 My friend / buy / a book /
of dramatic wildlife photos.
....

6 The local newspaper / print / colourful pictures /
of our school sports teams.
....

7 The photos / of the fire / look / fake.
....

Past continuous

**2 Complete the sentences with the Past
continuous form of these verbs.**

cry	have	look	play	~~talk~~	watch

1 Mrs Wilson *was talking* to her mother on the
phone.
2 Mrs Jones' baby .... in bed.
3 The young couple downstairs ....
a dull conversation.
4 Mr Smith .... an old-fashioned film
on TV.
5 The family .... an interesting game
of cards.
6 Dorian and Tom .... at photos.

**3 Make questions with the Past continuous.
Complete the answers with the correct verb.**

1 Dev / clean / his room / this morning?
Yes, he ....
*Was Dev cleaning his room this morning?
Yes, he was.*

2 you / take / photography lessons / last month
....
....
No, I ....

3 neighbours / tell / amusing stories /
last weekend?
....
....
Yes, they ....

4 Shane / make coffee / just now?
....
No, he ....

5 the girls / read / colourful magazines?
....
No, they ....

Past simple vs Past continuous

4 Complete the sentences with *when* or *while*.

1 Maria had a coffee *while* Max was doing the
shopping.
2 We were walking home .... we
saw the fire.
3 .... the plane landed, Elena was
waiting at the airport.
4 .... Richard was checking the
map, I got some petrol.

**5 Complete the conversations with the correct
form of the verbs.**

1 A What [1] *were you doing* (you/do) when I
[2]....................... (arrive) just now?
B Tammi [3]....................... (play) the piano and
we [4]....................... (paint) in the kitchen.
A I thought the phone [5]....................... (ring).
B I don't think so. We [6].......................
(not hear) anything.

2 A How [7]....................... (your brother/take)
this blurred photo of a horse?
B He [8]....................... (wait) for the right
moment, when someone [9].......................
(walk) into him.
A And then what [10]....................... (happen)?
B While I [11]....................... (help) him, the
horse [12]....................... (run away)!

Grammar Reference 3

Comparatives and Superlatives

Short adjectives	Comparatives	Superlatives
tall	taller (than)	the tallest
big	bigger (than)	the biggest
large	larger (than)	the largest
happy	happier (than)	the happiest

Long adjectives	Comparatives	Superlatives
popular	more popular (than)	the most popular
interesting	more interesting (than)	the most interesting

Irregular adjectives	Comparatives	Superlatives
good	better (than)	the best
bad	worse (than)	the worst

Use

- We use comparative adjectives to compare two people or things.
  *My hair is **longer** than Angela's.*
- We use superlative adjectives to compare one person or thing to others in a group.
  *Angela's got the **shortest** hair in the class.*

Form

Short adjectives	Comparatives	Superlatives
most adjectives:	add -er small → smaller	add the + -est small → the smallest
adjectives that end in one vowel + one consonant:	double the consonant and add -er fat → fatter	double the consonant and add the + -est fat → the fattest
adjectives that end in -e:	add -r nice → nicer	add the + -st nice → the nicest
adjectives that end in y:	drop the y and add -ier pretty → prettier	drop the y and add the + -iest pretty → the prettiest

Long adjectives	Comparatives	Superlatives
	add more boring → more boring	add the + most boring → the most boring

- After comparative adjectives we often use *than*.
  *Football is **more exciting than** tennis.*
- Before superlative adjectives we use *the*.
  *Jack is **the funniest** boy in the class.*

too and enough

The jeans are too expensive.
The jeans aren't cheap enough.
I haven't got enough money for the jeans.

Use

- We use *too* and *enough* to express an opinion about quantity (*too* = more than necessary, *not ... enough* = less than necessary).
  *It's **too** cold in here! Can you put the heating on?*
  *I'm **not** warm **enough**. Can you lend me a jumper?*

Form

- *too* goes before an adjective:
  *It's **too** hot in here!*
- *enough* goes after an adjective:
  *It's not cool **enough**.*
- *enough*, *too much* and *too many* go before a noun: **enough** time, **too much** milk, **too many** cars

much, many, a lot of

How much money has she got?	How many T-shirts has she got?
She's got a lot of money.	She's got a lot of T-shirts.
She hasn't got much/a lot of money.	She hasn't got many/a lot of T-shirts.
She's got too much money.	She's got too many T-shirts.

Use

- We use these words to talk about large quantities of things.
  *There were a **lot of** people/**many** cars in the street.*

Form

- We use *much* for uncountable nouns, and usually only in questions or the negative:
  *How **much** money does he have?*
  *She doesn't have **much** time.* (= She doesn't have a lot of time.)

- We use *many* for countable nouns, in the affirmative, negative and questions:
  *They have **many** pets in the house.*
  *They don't have **many** neighbours.*
  *How **many** friends does he have?*

Grammar practice

Comparatives and superlatives

1   **Put the words in the correct order.**

   1 know / most / person / the / He's / I / interesting
   He's the most interesting person I know.

   2 suitcase / than / This / I / is / thought / heavier
   ....

   3 here / home / weather / than / The / at / better / is
   ....

   4 class / She's / in / popular / the / girl / most / the
   ....

   5 car / new / old / than / is / better / the / Our / one
   ....

   6 world / cousin / person / My / the / is / in / funniest / the
   ....

2   **Make sentences with the comparative or superlative.**

   1 be / Poland / big / Spain?
   Is Poland bigger than Spain?

   2 be / German / difficult / English?
   ....

   3 Erika / tell / funny jokes / Brian.
   ....

   4 That cashpoint / far / this one!
   ....

   5 That café / have / bad sandwiches / in town!
   ....

   6 Japan / be / noisy / country / in the world.
   ....

   7 What / exciting film / to watch?
   ....

   8 That shop / have / expensive prices / in town.
   ....

too and *enough*

3   **Complete the conversation with *too* or *enough*.**

   A What did you do on holiday?
   B We went to the mountains.
   A How was the weather?
   B The first week it was [1] *too* hot to go out climbing, so we visited the town. The second week it was cool [2] .... to go out all day.
   A How about the food?
   B We ate out a lot. But one day we had trouble in the mountains because we didn't take [3] .... food. How about your holidays?
   A We went to Paris.
   B What was that like?
   A Mum wanted to go to the opera, but it was [4] .... expensive. Dad wanted to walk up the Eiffel Tower, but he didn't have [5] .... energy! I wanted to visit the Louvre, but it was [6] .... big to see everything in one day. There wasn't [7] .... time.
   B Yes, I know what you mean. Holidays are sometimes [8] .... tiring!

much, many, a lot of

4   **Complete the sentences with these words.**

a lot of	How many	How much
much	too many	~~too much~~

   1 I can't buy that shirt. It costs *too much*.
   2 .... apples would you like to buy?
   3 She's always very helpful, so she's got .... friends.
   4 I didn't sleep .... last night.
   5 .... did you spend on your laptop?
   6 I've got .... books for this shelf.

Present perfect

Regular verbs: affirmative		
I/You/We/They	've (have) cleaned	the house.
He/She/It	's (has) cleaned	

Regular verbs: negative		
I/You/We/They	haven't (have not) cleaned	the house.
He/She/It	hasn't (has not) cleaned	

Irregular verbs: affirmative		
I/You/We/They	've (have) done	the work.
He/She/It	's (has) done	

Irregular verbs: negative		
I/You/We/They	haven't (have not) done	the work.
He/She/It	hasn't (has not) done	

Regular verbs				
Have	I/you/we/they	ever	visited	Arizona?
Has	he/she/it			

Irregular verbs				
Have	I/you/we/they	ever	seen	a snake?
Has	he/she/it			

Short answers
Yes, I/you/we/they have. / No, I/you/we/they haven't.
Yes, he/she/it has. / No, he/she/it hasn't.

Use

We use the Present perfect to talk about:

- actions or events that happened at an unspecified time in the past.
  *John **has visited** China.* (but we don't know when)

- with *ever*, we ask questions about personal experiences.
  ***Have** you **ever listened** to a podcast?*

- with *never*, we talk about experiences we have not had.
  *No, I **haven't**. I**'ve never listened** to a podcast – but I**'ve visited** news websites!*

Present perfect vs Past simple

Present perfect	Past simple
A helicopter has landed in the jungle.	A plane crashed in the mountains *last Saturday*.
Have you ever seen a helicopter?	Did it crash because of the weather?
I've never flown in a helicopter.	Rescue teams located the plane on *Sunday morning*.

Use

We use the Past simple to talk about:

- actions or events that happened at a specific time in the past.

Time expressions

Present perfect: *ever, never, before, recently, in my life*
Past simple: *last night/week/year, five hours/days/months ago, in 2012*

Grammar practice

Present perfect

1 **Rewrite the sentences. Put the words in brackets in the correct place.**

1 Have you been to North America?   (ever)
Have you ever been to North America?

2 Which African countries he visited?   (has)
....
....

3 Has your brother something for the school blog?   (written)
....
....

4 We've watched a current affairs programme. (never)
....
....

5 They answered all today's emails.   (have)
....
....

6 I'm sorry, but I finished my report.   (haven't)
....
....

2 Write questions for the <u>underlined</u> answers.

1 He's made <u>some sandwiches</u>.
What has he made?

2 They've been to <u>France</u>.
....

3 I've won <u>a prize in the lottery</u>!
....

4 My aunt has had <u>a baby boy</u>!
....

5 Patricia's gone to <u>Italy</u>.
....

6 He's interviewed <u>Lady Gaga</u>.
....

7 We've finished reading <u>the news</u>.
....

8 They've written <u>an excellent report</u>.
....

Present perfect vs Past simple

3 Match the questions (1–6) to the answers (a–f).

1 Have you ever been to Madrid?   *f*
2 Have you ever written a blog?
3 Have you ever been on TV?
4 Have you ever recorded a podcast?
5 Have you ever bought a newspaper?
6 Have you ever watched the local news?

a Yes, I wrote a travel blog for my class trip in March.
b No, because I read the news on a website.
c Yes, I have. We recorded it in Science class.
d No, but my friend was on a talent show last year.
e Yes, I've seen it on TV and on my laptop.
f Yes, my family spent a weekend there last year.

4 Choose the correct options.

1 Kathy *has written /*(*wrote*) a letter to the newspaper last weekend.
2 That's my mum's new car. She *bought / has bought* it in March.
3 Where's Isabel? I *haven't seen / didn't see* her recently.
4 My parents *have gone / went* home half an hour ago.
5 Axel says he *never had / has never had* a pet.
6 What time *did you get up / have you got up* this morning?
7 I don't know this man! I *never met / 've never met* him before.

5 Write sentences.

1 I / go to / beach / but / I / never go to / mountains.
I've been to the beach but I've never been to the mountains.

2 In 2006 we / visit Scotland / and / write / travel blog.
....
....

3 We / download / podcast / but / not be / very interesting.
....
....

4 In Science class / we / write / three reports / this week.
....
....

5 Amy / interview / two local journalists / for the school magazine.
....
....

6 We read / headlines / on a news website / then / choose / a report to read.
....
....

6 Complete the conversation with the correct form of these verbs.

can not	catch	find		never hear
print	~~read~~	switch on		think

A ¹ *Have you read* this report in the paper?
B I don't know! What's it about?
A A man was out fishing in the sea one day when he ² .... a fish.
B And?
A On the way home, he ³ .... he heard some strange music in the car.
B Wasn't the car radio on?
A No! That's why he ⁴ .... understand where the music was from.
B So what happened?
A When he cut the fish open, he ⁵ .... an MP3 player in its stomach!
B That's impossible! I ⁶ .... such a silly story! ⁷ .... the fish .... the MP3 player??!
A This paper ⁸ .... some very strange reports recently.

Present perfect + *for* and *since*; *How long?*

How long **have we been here**?
We've been here for five days/a week/a month.

I **haven't read** a book since Saturday.

She's lived in France since 2010.

Use

We use the Present perfect with *for* to indicate a period of time:
*We'**ve been** on holiday **for** two weeks.*

We use the Present perfect with *since* to indicate a point in time:
*We'**ve been** on holiday **since** Monday the 14th.*

We use *How long?* to ask about the duration of an action:
***How long have you been** on holiday?*
***How long have you lived** here?*

Present perfect with *just*

You've just had an ice cream.

You've just missed the train.

The menu has just changed.

Use

We use the Present perfect with *just* to indicate an action that happened a short time ago:
*The six o'clock train **has just left**. (It's 6.03 now.)*
*I'**ve just been** to the bank. (Here's the money I got.)*

Grammar practice

Present perfect + *for* and *since*; *How long?*

1 **Choose the correct options.**
   1 We've lived here (for)/ since six years.
   2 I haven't heard that song for / since we were in Italy!
   3 I haven't visited Germany for / since a long time.
   4 Our families have gone camping together for / since we were young.
   5 It's been much warmer for / since the rain stopped.
   6 She's only had that toy for / since three weeks.

2 **Make sentences with the Present perfect and *for* or *since*.**
   1 Jared / not write / to his parents / March.
     Jared hasn't written to his parents since March.
   2 You / not tidy / room / weeks!
     ....
   3 Maria / not eat out / two years.
     ....
   4 The weather / be / very hot / the 15th.
     ....
   5 We / not stayed / in a hotel / October.
     ....
   6 Pablo / have to / stay in bed / five days.
     ....
   7 I / not put up / a tent / last summer.
     ....

3 Choose the correct options.

1 How (long) / many have you had your laptop?
2 How long / many days have you had a cold?
3 How long / many has Jane been in France?
4 How long / many times have you visited the castle?
5 How long / many have we had to wait?
6 How long / many letters have you sent?

4 Make questions for the underlined answers.

1 My mum has made four cakes for the party.
  How many cakes has your mum made for the party?

2 He's had to walk to school since the beginning of the month.
  ....

3 I've worked here for six weeks.
  ....

4 We've been abroad three times.
  ....

5 Your dad's been at the airport for three hours!
  ....

6 We've had our new car since last April.
  ....

Present perfect with *just*

5 Match the questions (1–6) to the answers (a–f).

1 Where are the postcards?   c
2 Is Kathy at home?
3 Am I in time for the film?
4 Is dinner ready?
5 Have you got my keys?
6 Are you ready to go?

a I've just put them back on the shelf.
b Yes! It's just started.
c I've just posted them.
d Yes! We've just packed our bags.
e I'm afraid she's just left.
f Your dad has just put it on the table!

6 Put the words in the correct order.

1 He's feeling happy because / has / good / he / news / had / just / some
  He's feeling happy because he has just had some good news.

2 She's feeling great because / has / test / passed / just / she / her
  ....
  ....

3 Mum's still a bit sleepy because / woken / just / she / up / has
  ....
  ....

4 My sister's really excited because / booked / has / she / a / just / holiday
  ....
  ....

5 Tim's tired because / kilometres / walked / has / he / just / ten
  ....
  ....

6 I feel really good because / been / I / just / to / have / the / gym
  ....
  ....

7 Andy's laughing because / good / heard / he / just / a / joke / has
  ....
  ....

have to/don't have to

Affirmative

I/You/We/They have to lay the table.
He/She/It has to lay the table.

Negative

I/You/We/They don't have to lay the table.
He/She/It doesn't have to lay the table.

Questions and short answers

Do you have to do any chores?
Yes, I do./No, I don't.
Does he have to do any chores?
Yes, he does./No, he doesn't.

Use

- We use *have to* when there is an obligation to do something.
  *I'm sorry, but we **have to leave** now.*
- We use *don't have to* when there is no obligation.
  *You **don't have to come** if you don't want to.*

must/mustn't

Affirmative and negative

I/You/He/She/It We/They	must listen	to her.
I/You/He/She/It We/They	mustn't (must not) listen	to her.

Use

- We use *must* when there is an obligation to do something.
  *You **must take** your medicine now!*
  *In the UK, you **must drive** on the left.*
- We use *mustn't* to express prohibition: an obligation NOT to do something.
  *You **mustn't wear** shoes inside a mosque.*
  *You **mustn't take** photographs inside the museum.*

Predictions with *will, won't, might*

Definite

I think she'll be relieved.
You won't have any problems, I'm sure.
Will they finish it?

Possible

I might see them tomorrow. I'm not sure.
He might not like the film.

Use

- We use *will/won't* to express what we think of as a definite future.
  *I'm sure they**'ll be** very happy.*
  *We**'ll** never **forget** you!*
  *There **won't be** much traffic in the morning.*
- We use *might* to express what we think of as only possible, but not definite.
  *If you're here tomorrow, I **might see** you in the library.*
  *We **might not go** out if the weather's bad.*

Grammar practice

have to/don't have to, must/mustn't

1   **Make sentences with the correct form of *have to/don't have to*.**

   1 Sue can't go out because she / have / study.
   Sue can't go out because she has to study.

   2 What chores do I / have to / do next weekend?
   ....

   3 Did you / have to / work late / last night?
   ....

   4 They're staying in a hotel, so they / not have to / cook / meals.
   ....

   5 Do / we / have to / wear / suits for the wedding tomorrow?
   ....

   6 Phil got up early, so I / not have to / wake him up.
   ....

2 Complete the conversation with the correct form of *have to*.

A What's it like at your summer camp?
B Some things are the same as at home. We ¹*have to* get up early and we ²......................... make the bed. But we ³......................... do all the activities, because we can usually choose.
A That sounds OK! What about meals? ⁴......................... (you) cook?
B No, we don't. There's a specific activity in the morning if you want to learn.
A And at night, what time ⁵......................... (you) go to bed?
B Officially, we ⁶......................... switch off the lights at midnight, but most of us sit and chat in the dark until much later.

3 Life in the army. Look at the table. Write sentences with *mustn't, have to/don't have to*. (O = Obligation, N/O = No obligation, P = Prohibition).

1	get up late	P
2	sweep the floors	O
3	wash uniforms	N/O
4	iron uniforms	O
5	cook meals	P
6	do physical exercise	O
7	speak English	N/O

1 They *mustn't get up late.*
2 They...
3 They...
4 They...
5 They...
6 They...
7 They...

Predictions with *will, won't, might*

4 Complete the sentences with *will, won't* or *might*.

1 Tom is sick so he *won't* be at class today.
2 The weather is very changeable so you .... need an umbrella.
3 .... you bring me a souvenir from Sweden?
4 Jessie's in the garden so she .... (not) hear you.
5 There's been a lot of snow so it .... take longer to get home today.

5 Write sentences with *will, won't* or *might* and the words in brackets.

1 I / not think / Sheila / go / to the theatre. (will)
   I don't think Sheila will go to the theatre.
2 Tamara / be / very upset, / so / she not go out tonight. (won't)
   ....
   ....
3 Rob / invite you / to the party / if / you ask him nicely! (might)
   ....
   ....
4 Where / you be / at five o'clock / tomorrow afternoon? (will)
   ....
   ....
5 Diana / be / very clever, / but / she not know / the answer! (might)
   ....
   ....
6 Terry / look / tired, / but / he not give up! (won't)
   ....
   ....

be going to

Affirmative

There are going to be 200 elephant sculptures.
The charity is going to make elephant corridors.

Negative

There aren't going to be 200 elephant sculptures.
The charity isn't going to make elephant corridors.

Questions and short answers

Are they going to make them?
Yes, they are./No, they aren't.
What are they going to do?

Use

We use *be going to* in order to express some kind of future intention or plan:
We're going to have skiing lessons this winter.
I'm not going to practise piano today because I don't have time.

will or be going to

Predictions

In 30 years there won't be any Asian elephants.
You'll probably meet one in town this weekend.

Plans or intentions

We're going to save the Asian elephant.

Use

We use *will* to express a prediction:
You'll find the spoons in the drawer next to the cooker.
Carmen will probably study chemistry.

We often use *will* after these expressions:
I think/I don't think, I'm sure/I'm not sure, maybe, perhaps.

First conditional

if + Present simple, will + infinitive

If we don't protest, they will close the library.

will ('ll) + verb > if + Present simple

They will close the library if we don't protest.

Use

We use the First conditional to talk about possible situations. We feel these situations have a real chance of happening if the condition comes true:
*If you **don't hurry up**, we'll miss the bus.*
*If it **rains** today, we'll stay at home.*

Form

If + Present simple, will + infinitive:
If the weather **is** good, we'll go swimming.

will + infinitive if + Present simple:
We'll go swimming **if** the weather **is** good.

Grammar practice

be going to

1 **Put the words in the correct order.**

1 A going / dinner / are / to / you / have / What / for / ?
What are you going to have for dinner ?
B Probably just some fruit and yoghurt.

2 A put / Where / mirror / her / going / is / Jane / to / new / ?
....
B I think it's for her bedroom.

3 A are / tattoo / you / to / Why / get / going / a / ?
....
B Because it's fashionable!

4 A theatre / the / When / going / to / are / they / open / new / ?
....
B Some time in September, I think.

will or *be going to*

2 **Choose the correct options.**

1 David isn't sure about the bus. Perhaps *he 's going to / (he'll)* take the train.
2 We like this place! *We're going to / We'll* stay three more days.
3 Ana has to work just now. Maybe *she's going to / she'll* join us later.
4 He's just bought the tickets. *They're going to / They'll* travel on Monday.
5 They're flying to Mexico. I'm sure *they're going to / they'll* have a wonderful time.
6 I'm not feeling very well, so *I'm going to / I'll take* an aspirin.

3 **Complete the conversation with the correct form of *will* or *going to*.**

A What are your plans for the bank holiday?
B We ¹ *'re going to* have a special dinner with the family.
A What's on the menu?
B I'm sure Mum ² .... cook turkey. It's her speciality. But later maybe we ³ .... have a special dessert, because I'd like to try something different. And you?
A We ⁴ .... travel to the city to surprise my brother.
B That'll be fun.
A Yes. He's been working really hard and hasn't been able to get home. He ⁵ .... probably be really happy to see us.
B That ⁶ .... be nice!

First conditional

4 **Make sentences.**

1 If you don't practise enough, you / never / play well!
If you don't practise enough, you'll never play well!
2 If we buy one of these, we / get / another one free.
....
....
3 If you open this box, you / find / a surprise inside.
....
....
4 We'll catch the six o'clock bus if / we / be / lucky!
....
....
5 You'll probably get that information if / you / look / on the internet.
....
....
6 I'll be very surprised if / Steve / not be / at home.
....
....

5 **Complete the replies with the correct form of the verbs.**

1 A What are you laughing about?
  B If I *tell* (tell) you, *will you keep* (you/keep) it secret?
2 A I can't do my homework!
  B If I .... (help) you, ... (you/take) the dog for a walk?
3 A I don't like this food!
  B If you .... (not finish) your food, you .... (not get) any dessert!
4 A We're leaving tomorrow!
  B .... (you/call) me if I .... (give) you my phone number?
5 A This house is a mess!
  B .... (you/do) the ironing if I .... (vacuum) the floor?
6 A Romeo's gone!
  B What .... (Juliet/do) if he .... (not come) back?

Second conditional

> **if + Past simple, would ('d) + verb**
> **would ('d) + verb > if + Past simple**

Affirmative

If I had a normal job, I'd be bored.

Negative

If I wasn't a stuntwoman, I'd do extreme sports.
If I was scared, I wouldn't be a stuntwoman.

Questions and short answers

Would you be happier if you had a normal job?
Yes, I would./No, I wouldn't.

Use

We use the Second conditional to talk about
unlikely/unreal situations. We feel these situations
have very little chance of happening, because
the condition itself is nearly impossible. The Past
simple tense expresses this near impossibility.
*If I **had** the money, I'**d buy** a castle.*
*We'**d stay** longer, if we **had** the time.*

Form

If + Past simple, would + infinitive.
*If the weather **was** good, we'**d go** swimming.*
would + infinitive if + Past simple.
*We'**d go** swimming if the weather **was** good.*

Relative pronouns

> It's the place where I play football.
> She's the woman who was in the car.
> That's the cat which was under a car.

Use

We use relative pronouns to identify people/places/
things, or to give more information about them:
*That's the guide **who** showed us the city.*
*This is the hotel **where** we stayed.*
*These are the souvenirs **which** we bought for the
family.*
*It's an object **which** we use to open doors. (= a key)*
*It's a place **where** you can relax and enjoy yourself.*
(= a holiday resort)
*She's the kind of person **who** can tell you lots of
stories. (= grandmother)*

Grammar practice

Second conditional

1 **Put the words in the correct order.**
What would happen if …
1 off / bus / school / at / didn't / the / get / I / ?
I didn't get off the bus at school?
2 Saturdays / to / had / we / go / on / school /
to / ?
....
3 with / man / the / spy / newspaper / was / the /
a / ?
....

If I didn't take the bus, …
4 bike / school / by / to / go / could / I
....
5 time / get / on / wouldn't / school / to / I
....
6 rain / to / have / would / the / I / to / walk / in /
school
....

2 **Make sentences.**
1 If I were you, I / not do that again.
If I were you, I wouldn't do that again.
2 If this story was true, we / all be /
in serious trouble!
....
....
3 If Dad saw you now, he / not believe his eyes!
....
....
4 They'd have to go to hospital if his temperature /
not go down.
....
....
5 I'd ask for a refund if my flight / be cancelled.
....
....
6 I wouldn't believe him if I / not know him!
....
....

3 Complete the replies with the correct form of the verbs.

1 A So you're going to be late?
  B Sorry! If there *was* (be) an earlier train, we*'d get* (get) there in time.

2 A Will Uncle Jack remember it's my birthday?
  B I .... (be) very surprised if he .... (not send) you a present.

3 A I don't know what to do!
  B If I .... (be) you, I .... (ask) your father for some ideas.

4 A You've got too much luggage!
  B I know. If I .... (have) a car, it .... (not be) a problem.

5 A Can you see the animals over there?
  B It .... (be) much easier if there .... (not be) so many trees!

6 A Are you enjoying the walk?
  B It .... (not be) so difficult if the path .... (not be) so narrow.

Relative pronouns

4 Complete the conversation with *who*, *which*, or *where*.

A Haven't you seen these photos before?
B No, I haven't.
A Well this is my classmate ¹ *who* had to go home with a temperature.
B OK. And this?
A That's the Science room ² .... two students got burns in an experiment.
B How did that happen?
A They were using equipment ³ .... didn't work properly.
B Who's that girl there?
A She's the one ⁴ .... got a rash from touching frogs in the Biology class.
B Yes, that happened to a friend of mine, too. He played with some cats ⁵ .... lived near the beach and his hands went all red.
A Is that the beach ⁶ .... we were on holiday this summer?
B No, it's a different one.

5 Make sentences with *who*, *which*, or *where*.

1 This is a photo / the accident / I have / when I / be ten.
  This is a photo of the accident which I had when I was ten.

2 This is the park / it happen.
  ....

3 These are the skates / I be / wearing.
  ....

4 Here's the doctor / put the plaster / on my arm.
  ....
  ....

5 This is the café / my father / buy / me an ice cream.
  ....
  ....

6 This is the nurse / write / a message on my plaster.
  ....
  ....

Present simple passive

Affirmative
It is made with plastic tubes. They are made with plastic.

Negative
The machine isn't made with plastic. Gloves aren't usually used to climb walls.

Questions and short answers
Is the machine made with plastic? Yes, it is./No, it isn't. Are the gloves used to climb walls? Yes, they are./No, they aren't.

Use

We use the passive when we want to focus more on an action than on the person or thing doing the action:
*Coffee **is produced** in many different countries.*

Form

subject + Present simple of *be* + past participle of the main verb
Coffee is produced *in tropical countries.*
Coffee is not produced *in cold countries.*
Is coffee produced *in Africa? Yes, it is.*

Past simple passive

Affirmative	Negative
It was made by Ella.	It wasn't made by Ella.
They were bought yesterday.	The instructions weren't included in the box.

Questions and short answers	
Was it made from a tin can? Yes, it was./No, it wasn't. Were the instructions included? Yes, they were./No, they weren't.	

Form

subject + Past simple of *be* + past participle of the main verb
The first cars were made *in the late 1800s.*
Cars were not built *before the late 1800s.*
Were the first cars made *in Europe? Yes, they were.*

Active and passive

Active
Blind people use Braille. You write messages on a keyboard.

Passive
Braille is used by blind people. Messages are written on a keyboard.

Use

We use **active** forms when the person or thing doing the action is important:
Some people in Ireland speak Gaelic.

We use **passive** forms when we consider the action is more important than the person or thing doing the action:
*Gaelic **is spoken** in Ireland.* (= this is where we find Gaelic)
*Many buildings **were destroyed** in this city.* (= an important fact)

Sometimes we also want to specify the person or thing doing the action:
*Gaelic **is spoken by some people** in Ireland.* (= not everyone speaks the language)
*Many buildings **were destroyed by** fire.* (= fire and not water or other causes)

Most often, however, the person or thing doing the action is not mentioned:
*Video games **are produced** in Japan.*
*Houses in this area **are built** of wood or brick.*

Grammar practice

Present simple passive

1 **Complete the sentences with the Present simple passive form of the verbs.**

   1 Our computers *are packed* (pack) in this department here.
   2 The keyboard .... (attach) to the case.
   3 The electric cables .... (add) in a separate box.
   4 The battery .... (produce) in a different factory.
   5 The sockets .... (test) by that department there.
   6 The remote control .... (sell) separately.

2 Make questions with the Present simple passive.

1 Where / cables / plug in?
Where are the cables plugged in?

2 How / this tube / produce?

....

3 What kind of keyboard / use / in China?

....

4 How / the sockets / add?

....

5 When / the battery / attach?

....

6 Where / these engines / build?

....

Past simple passive

3 Make sentences with the Past simple passive.

1 Horses / domesticate / over 6,000 years ago.
Horses were domesticated over 6,000 years ago.

2 Modern bicycles / not invent / until about 1885.

....
....

3 The first car factory / build / in Germany in 1885.

....
....

4 City bus services / begin / in England and France in the 1820s.

....
....

5 The first railway trains / run in England in the 1820s.

....
....

6 The first aeroplanes / not fly / until 1903.

....
....

4 Complete the questions with the Past simple passive form of the verbs.

1 When *was* the local theme park *opened*? (open)

2 Where .... the *Twilight* films .... ? (make)

3 When .... the baby .... to its father in *Ice Age 1*? (return)

4 How .... Princess Fiona .... by Shrek? (rescue)

5 When .... the ring .... into the volcano in the *Lord of the Rings*? (throw)

6 Where .... *High School Musical* .... ? (film)

Active and passive

5 Change these active sentences into passive sentences. Include *by* + noun only if necessary.

1 People make flour from wheat.
Flour is made from wheat.

2 The school theatre group performed this play.

....
....

3 Someone in France writes this blog.

....
....

4 The local factory produces one thousand cars a week.

....
....

5 Mark Zuckerberg created a huge social network.

....
....

6 A monkey stole our sandwiches!

....
....

7 Three boys discovered some old coins in a field.

....
....

Home Sweet Home
Unit vocabulary

1 **Translate the words.**

Rooms and parts of the house

attic ....
balcony ....
ceiling ....
cellar ....
drive ....
fireplace ....
floor ....
garage ....
hall ....
landing ....
lawn ....
office ....
patio ....
roof ....
stairs ....
wall ....

2 **Translate the words.**

Furniture and household objects

alarm clock ....
armchair ....
blind ....
bookcase ....
chest of drawers ....
curtains ....
cushions ....
duvet ....
mirror ....
pillow ....
rug ....
vase ....
wardrobe ....

Vocabulary extension

3 **Match the photos to these words. Use your dictionary if necessary. Write the words in English and your language.**

chimney   lift   taps   ~~towel~~   washbasin

1 ....
....

2 ....
....

3 ....
....

4 .... *towel* ....
....

5 ....
....

Vocabulary 2

What's The Story
Unit vocabulary

1 Translate the words.

Adjectives to describe pictures

amusing ....

blurred ....

colourful ....

dark ....

dramatic ....

dull ....

fake ....

horrible ....

interesting ....

lovely ....

old-fashioned ....

silly ....

2 Translate the words.

Adjective + preposition

afraid of ....

angry with ....

bad at ....

bored with ....

excited about ....

good at ....

interested in ....

keen on ....

popular with ....

proud of ....

sorry for ....

tired of ....

Vocabulary extension

3 Match the photos to these words. Use your dictionary if necessary. Write the words in English and your language.

annoyed about	~~disappointed with~~	mysterious
scary	surprised at	

1 ....
....

2 ....
....

3 ......*disappointed with*......
....

4 ....
....

5 ....
....

Vocabulary 3

It's A Bargain!

Unit vocabulary

1 Translate the words.

Shopping nouns

bargain ....

cashpoint ....

change ....

coin ....

customer ....

high street ....

market stall ....

note ....

price ....

products ....

queue ....

sale ....

shop assistant ....

shopping basket ....

stallholder ....

2 Translate the words.

Money verbs

afford ....

borrow ....

buy ....

cost ....

earn ....

lend ....

pay by credit card ....

pay in cash ....

save ....

sell ....

spend ....

win ....

Vocabulary extension

3 Match the photos to these words. Use your dictionary if necessary. Write the words in English and your language.

bar code   discount   receipt   refund   ~~sell-by date~~

1 ....

2 ....

3 ....*sell-by date*........... ....

4 ....

5 ....

Vocabulary 4

In The News
Unit vocabulary

1 Translate the words.

News and media

blog ....
current affairs programme
....
headline ....
international news ....
interview (v) ....
journalist ....
local news ....
national news ....
news flash ....
newspaper ....
news presenter ....
news website ....
podcast ....
report (v, n) ....

2 Translate the words.

Adverbs of manner

angrily ....
badly ....
carefully ....
carelessly ....
early ....
fast ....
happily ....
hard ....
late ....
loudly ....
patiently ....
quietly ....
sadly ....
slowly ....
well ....

Vocabulary extension

3 Match the photos and pictures to these words. Use your dictionary if necessary. Write the words in English and your language.

cartoon strip	entertainments guide	front page
proudly	~~quickly~~	

1 ....
....

2 ....
....

3 ....
....

4 .... *quickly* ....
....

5 ....
....

Happy Holidays

Unit vocabulary

1 **Translate the words.**

Holidays

book a holiday ....

buy souvenirs ....

check into a hotel ....

eat out ....

get a tan ....

get lost ....

go abroad ....

go camping ....

lose your luggage ....

pack your bag ....

put up a tent ....

see the sights ....

stay in a hotel ....

write a travel blog ....

2 **Translate the words.**

Meanings of *get*

arrive (*get to the campsite*)

....

become (*get cold*) ....

buy (*get a key ring*)

....

fetch (*get the suntan lotion*)

....

receive (*get a postcard*)

....

walk/move (*get on the bus*)

....

Vocabulary extension

3 **Match the photos to these words. Use your dictionary if necessary. Write the words in English and your language.**

book bed and breakfast	buy a travel pass	get a taxi
get sunburnt	~~stay at a youth hostel~~	

1 ....*stay at a youth hostel*....

....

2 ....

....

3 ....

....

4 ....

....

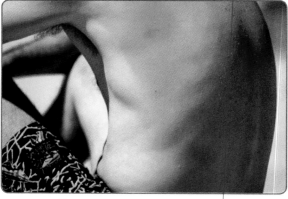

5 ....

....

Vocabulary 6

That's Life!
Unit vocabulary

1 **Translate the words**

Household chores

clear the table ....
cook a meal ....
do the ironing ....
do the washing-up ....
feed the cat ....
hang out the washing
....
lay the table ....
load the dishwasher ....
make your bed ....
mow the lawn ....
run the washing machine
....
sweep the floor ....
take out the rubbish ....
walk the dog ....
wash the car ....
vacuum the floor ....

2 **Translate the words.**

Feelings adjectives

confident ....
confused ....
disappointed ....
embarrassed ....
fed up ....
glad ....
grateful ....
guilty ....
jealous ....
lonely ....
nervous ....
relaxed ....
relieved ....
upset ....

Vocabulary extension

3 Match the photos to these words. Use your dictionary if necessary. Write the words in English and your language.

~~anxious~~   carefree   change the bed
mop the floor   water the plants

1 ....
....

2 ....
....

3 ....
....

4 ...._anxious_............
....

5 ....
....

Make A Difference
Unit vocabulary

1   **Translate the words.**

Protest and support

banner ....
charity ....
collection ....
demonstration ....
donation ....
fundraising event ....
march ....
petition ....
placard ....
sit-in ....
slogan ....
volunteer ....

2   **Translate the words.**

Verb + preposition

agree with ....
apologise for ....
argue with ....
believe in ....
care about ....
decide on ....
disapprove of ....
hope for ....
insist on ....
know about ....
protest against ....
worry about ....

Vocabulary extension

3   **Match the photos to these words. Use your dictionary if necessary. Write the words in English and your language.**

campaign for/against   ~~endangered species~~   hand in
human rights   minority group

1 ....
....

2 ....
....

3 .... *endangered species* ....
....

4 ....
....

5 ....
....

Danger And Risk
Unit vocabulary

1 Translate the words.

Extreme adjectives

awful ....

boiling ....

brilliant ....

exhausted ....

freezing ....

furious ....

huge ....

terrifying ....

thrilled ....

tiny ....

2 Translate the words.

Illness and injury

a burn ....

a cold ....

a cough ....

a cut ....

a headache ....

a rash ....

a sore throat ....

a sprained ankle ....

a stomachache ....

a temperature ....

backache ....

toothache ....

Vocabulary extension

3 Match the photos to these words. Use your dictionary if necessary. Write the words in English and your language.

bandage   delighted   ~~horrified~~   needle   plaster

1 ....
....

2 .... *horrified* ....
....

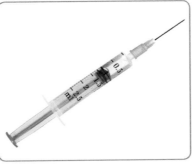

3 ....
....

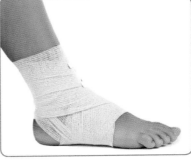

4 ....
....

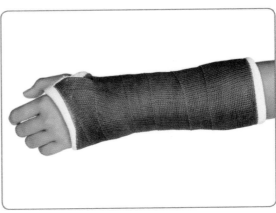

5 ....
....

Inventions

Unit vocabulary

1 Translate the words.

Machine nouns and verbs

Verbs

attach ....

build ....

communicate ....

invent ....

press ....

plug in ....

produce ....

switch off ....

switch on ....

Nouns

battery ....

button ....

cable ....

keyboard ....

remote control ....

socket ....

tube ....

wheel ....

2 Translate the words.

Word building

build – builder – building
....

design – designer – design
....

invent – inventor – invention
....

paint – painter – painting
....

produce – producer – product
....

write – writer – writing
....

Vocabulary extension

3 Match the photos to these words. Use your dictionary if necessary. Write the words in English and your language.

composer	enter key	function key	sale	~~unplug~~

1 ....*unplug*...........
....

2 ....
....

3 ....
....

4 ....
....

5 ....
....

Speaking and Listening 1

Describing a place

Speaking

1 🔊 **42** **Complete the text with these phrases. Then listen and check.**

big fireplace	big windows	comfortable
~~quite new~~	very narrow	wardrobe
wooden ceilings		

Welcome to the old castle! This is the main entrance, between these two towers. The towers look a bit strange because many parts of them are ¹*quite new*. The windows are ² .... and they don't have any glass. If we go inside, we can see the main buildings on the left. The building with the really ³ .... is the Great Hall. It has six fireplaces and tables and chairs for a hundred people! The building opposite the Hall is for the royal apartments. The apartments have high ⁴ ...., walls covered in special cloths called tapestries and rugs on the floor. Each room has a ⁵ .... to keep people warm and of course, a very ⁶ .... bed. There isn't very much furniture, usually just a chest of drawers and a ⁷ ....

2 🔊 **43** **Complete the conversation with these phrases. Then listen and check.**

bit small	~~like~~	original
uncomfortable	very expensive	what

A What's that new café ¹*like*?
B Do you mean the 'Skyspace'?
A Yes, that's it. I've heard it has some really ² .... decoration.
B Yes, that's what Celia says, too. She told me it's got a blue ceiling with stars painted on it.
A Wow! So ³ .... are the tables and chairs like?
B The tables are painted yellow like the sun, but they're a ⁴ ....
A OK!
B And the chairs look like stars, but they're quite ⁵ ....
A Right. And what about the prices?
B Celia says they're ⁶ .... It costs €3 for a coffee, for example.
A OK, forget that! We'll go to the café at the station.

Listening

3 🔊 **44** **Listen and complete the sentences.**
1 Laura is staying in a hotel on the ....
2 She's going on holiday with her ....
3 Frank and Laura can see the hotel in some ....
4 The rooms have a .... with a table and chairs.
5 Frank isn't interested in playing .... at this kind of hotel.
6 Frank doesn't like playing .... at school.
7 There's a .... disco at the hotel.

4 🔊 **44** **Listen again. Who says these phrases? Write F for Frank or L for Laura.**
1 What's it like?   ....
2 look at the view!   ....
3 four tennis courts   ....
4 Not at school!   ....
5 What about nightlife?   ....
6 That sounds like fun!   ....

Speaking and Listening 2

Permission

Speaking

1   🔊 45   **Match the questions (1–6) to the answers (a–f). Then listen and check.**

1 Can I stay overnight at Marta's house?   *c*
2 Do you mind if we park here?
3 Is it OK if I wear jeans?
4 Can we invite some friends for the weekend?
5 Do you mind if I come home late?
6 Is it OK if we make pizza?

a No, I'm afraid it isn't. You need something more formal.
b No, I don't mind. But not later than eleven o'clock.
c Yes, you can. But call me in the morning.
d Go ahead! I'll have one with four cheeses.
e No, you can't. We're going away this weekend.
f I'm afraid I do! This is the entrance to a garage!

2   🔊 46   **Complete the conversation with these phrases. Then listen and check.**

Can we do	Do you mind	~~Go ahead~~
I'm afraid	take photos	Yes, of course

A Bankside Holiday Apartments! Can I help you?
B I'd like to ask a few questions, please.
A ¹*Go ahead*!
B Is it OK if we ²......................... of the apartment?
A ³......................... ! Most people take holiday pictures.
B That's fine! And what about uploading them on the internet? ⁴......................... that?
A Yes, that's not a problem.
B Right! And what about pets? ⁵......................... if we bring a pet?
A What kind of pet? ⁶......................... we can't accept large animals.
B It's just a cat.
A Yes, that's OK, but only on the balcony.
B Thank you!

Listening

3   🔊 47   **Listen and choose the correct options.**

1 The mother is (happy)/ unhappy for the boy to see the photos.
2 The photos are in *a box / an album*.
3 The grandmother died in *1970 / 1980*.
4 The grandparents were born *before / after* the war.
5 The *grandfather / grandmother* was an electrician.

4   🔊 47   **Listen again. Put the phrases in the order you hear them.**

a in those days   ....
b might get lost   ....
c When were they alive?   ....
d just before   ....
e have a look at   .1..

Asking for help

Speaking

1 🔊 **48** **Put the sentences in the correct order. Then listen and check.**

a Three. What do you think of this one? ....

b Well, can you hold these ones while I try the other ones? ....

c Yes, I think so, too. ....

d Lisa! Could you give me a hand with these shirts? .1..

e It looks too big for you, actually. ....

f Sure. What do you want me to do? ....

g OK! How many have you got? ....

2 🔊 **49** **Complete the conversation with these words. Then listen and check.**

can't	cost	~~give~~	lending
price	looking	No	

A Jerzy! Could you ¹*give* me a hand at the market? I don't speak much Polish!

B ²...................... problem! What are you ³...................... for?

A Some T-shirts, I think.

B OK. Do you see any that you like?

A Those ones look all right. Could you ask how much they ⁴...................... ?

B Sure. The stallholder says they're €10 each.

A That's a good ⁵...................... ! I'll take five of them, but in different colours.

B That's easy. There you are!

A Oh dear! I've only got €30! I forgot to go to the bank! Would you mind ⁶...................... me €20 to pay for the T-shirts?

B Sorry, I ⁷...................... ! I didn't bring my wallet. But there's a cashpoint just round the corner. We can go there.

A OK, let's do that!

Listening

3 🔊 **50** **Listen and choose the correct options.**

1 The girl needs help with her *housework /* ⟨*homework*⟩.

2 The group *can / can't* afford hotels.

3 The problem with camping is the *location / weather*.

4 The best alternative is *camping / youth hostels*.

5 The girl *has got / hasn't got* her mobile phone just now.

4 🔊 **50** **Listen again. Put the phrases in the order you hear them.**

a Could you think of a better way? ....

b she forgot to bring it back ....

c Everyone can afford that! ....

d Check how much you have to pay ....

e Are you busy? .1..

f I'll check that now. ....

Speaking and Listening 4

Doubt and disbelief
Speaking

1 🔊 **51** **Put the sentences in the correct order. Then listen and check.**

a What are you reading? ..1..
b And what does it say? ....
c Let me check. Oops! I've sent 45! ....
d It says that high school students send about 30 text messages a day. ....
e A magazine report about young people and mobile phones. ....
f I don't believe it! I've only sent about 20 messages today. And you? ....

2 🔊 **52** **Complete the conversation with these phrases. Then listen and check.**

a strange figure	~~believe~~	impossible
joking	just a statue	No, really
That's strange		

A Have you read this report about a ghost in the local museum?
B I don't ¹ *believe* it!
A It's been in the national news as well.
B ² .... ? What's the story?
A It says people have seen ³ .... in the museum. And that there have been reports like this for many years.
B Well, I've never heard of them! Does the figure move or is it ⁴ .... ?
A They say it moves round different parts of the museum.
B That's ⁵ .... You would see it on the video cameras!
A But there aren't any video cameras!
B ⁶ .... Most museums have them. Listen! Why don't we spend the night there with a camera?
A You're ⁷ .... ! They wouldn't let us do that!

Listening

3 🔊 **53** **Listen and match the key words (1–5) to words (a–e).**

1 vampire — a dates
2 Germany b Happy Birthday
3 lose c semi-finals
4 dog d trailer
5 concert e match

4 🔊 **53** **Listen again. Put the phrases in the order you hear them.**

a What about France? ....
b You're joking! ....
c Anything else? ....
d I don't know. ....
e I expected that! ..1..
f I don't believe it! ....

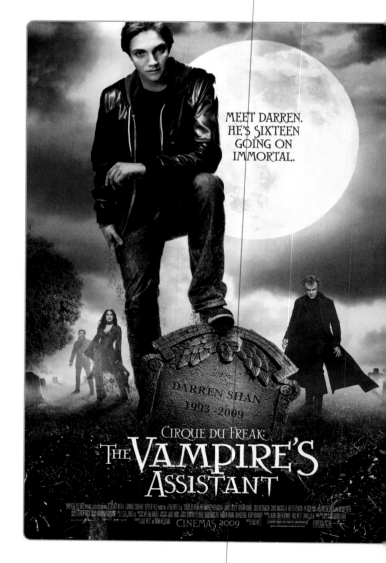

Asking for information

Speaking

1 🔊 **54** **Put the words in order. Then listen and check.**

A ¹ me / Excuse / us / Can / help / you / . / ?

Excuse me. Can you help us?

B Sure!

A ² to / T-shirts / good / a / Where's / buy / place / ?

....

B There's a souvenir shop near the station.

A ³ can / there / get / we / How / ?

....

B It's a five-minute walk.

A ⁴ there / money / there / get / a / bank / to / Is / ?

....

B There's one inside the station.

A ⁵ take / zoo / How / get / does / to / long / it / the / to / ?

....

B About fifteen minutes by bus.

2 🔊 **55** **Complete the conversation with these phrases. Then listen and check.**

a bit far	About twenty minutes
~~for a long time~~	here you are
not too expensive	over there
The best way	

A Excuse me! Can you help us? We're looking for the zoo.

B The zoo? I haven't been there ¹ *for a long time*! Have you got a map?

A Yes, ² ....

B OK, let's see. This is where we are now, and that's the zoo ³ ....

A Is it far?

B It's ⁴ .... , yes.

A How can we get there?

B ⁵ .... is probably by bus. There's a bus every quarter of an hour.

A How long does it take?

B ⁶ ....

A Is there a good place to eat at the zoo?

B Yes, it's got a cafeteria somewhere and it's ⁷ ....

A Thank you very much. That's really helpful!

Listening

3 🔊 **56** **You will hear four conversations. Match the conversations (1–4) to the topics (a–d).**

a the beach ....

b an art gallery ..1..

c sunglasses ....

d a theme park ....

4 🔊 **56** **Listen again. Are the sentences true (T) or false (F)?**

Conversation 1

1 Speaker 2 can't answer the question. *T*

Conversation 2

2 Speaker 1 prefers the taxi. ....

Conversation 3

3 Speaker 2 prefers the shop in the high street. ....

Conversation 4

4 There's a bus every fifteen minutes. ....

Giving advice
Speaking

1 **● 57 Put the conversation in the correct order. Then listen and check.**

a What's the matter? Is there anything
I can do? .1..

b Well why don't you look in the car then? ....

c Did you come home on the bus yesterday? ....

d Maybe you should check your room. ....

e That's a good idea! I didn't think about
that. Thanks! ....

f No, my mum drove me home. ....

g I've lost Jill's present. She'll be really upset! ....

h I've looked there three times! ....

2 **● 58 Complete the conversation with these phrases. Then listen and check.**

don't have to	I won't see	Why don't you
you should let	~~you should worry~~	

A You don't look very happy! What's the
problem?

B I've just found out that Sheryl's having a party
and she hasn't invited me!

A I don't think ¹*you should worry* about that.
Other people have parties as well.

B Yes, but Olga's going and if I can't go,
² .... her!

A OK, I understand. But you ³ .... go
to a party to see her.

B Yes, but we've got very different timetables at
school.

A ⁴ .... just ask Sheryl for an
invitation?

B I'd be too embarrassed!

A All right, maybe ⁵ .... me ask her
then.

B Will you?

A Sure. Anything for a friend!

B Thanks!

Listening

3 **● 59 Listen to the conversation. Choose the correct options.**

1 The *boy / girl* is fed up.

2 The girl has to look after *her / her brother's* dog.

3 She has to *feed and wash / feed and walk*
the dog.

4 The boy offers the girl *one solution /
two solutions* to the problem.

5 The boy has a *cat / dog*.

4 **● 59 Listen again. Who says these phrases? Write B for the boy or G for the girl.**

1 What's new? .B.

2 What's the matter? ....

3 It's not fair! ....

4 just tell me ....

5 That's great ....

Persuading

Speaking

1 ◯ 60 **Put the words in the correct order. Then listen and check.**

A Let's go and make a collection. Come on.
¹ fun / It'll / be / ! /
It'll be fun!

B I'm not so sure about that.

A I don't really want to design banners for you.

B ² better / It's / doing / nothing / than / !
....

A But we don't know how to make placards.

B ³ can / quickly / sure / we / I'm / learn
....

A What about a petition?

B ⁴ know / idea / I / if / good / that's / a / don't
....

A I'm sure you'll do a great job.

B ⁵ it / do / OK, / I'll / !
....

2 ◯ 61 **Complete the conversation with these phrases. Then listen and check.**

I don't know	~~If I paint the slogans~~
I'm not sure about	it'll be fun
it's better than	

A We need to make some placards for next weekend!

B Who's 'we', Dad?

A You and me, of course.

B But it's your sit-in, Dad. You're organising it.

A And if I lose my job, you won't get any pocket money! ¹ *If I paint the slogans*, will you cut the wood?

B ² .... , Dad.

A Come on, ³ .... to work together!

B But you know I'm allergic to sawdust!

A I know that you say you're allergic! OK, I'll cut the wood, but you'll have to paint the slogans!

B ⁴ .... that.

A Well, ⁵ .... walking home after your party tonight, isn't it?

B All right, you win. I'll do it!

Listening

3 ◯ 62 **Listen to the conversation and complete the summary. Use one word in each space.**

The girl wants her mother to go to a
¹ *fundraising* event with her. She wants to help a
² .... , but her mother doesn't really
³ .... to go. The mother wants the girl
to help her ⁴ .... the beds, but the girl
⁵ .... like that idea. In the end, the
mother ⁶ .... the girl to help, and they
both go out together.

4 ◯ 62 **Listen again. Who says these phrases? Write M for mother or D for daughter.**

1 a bit busy   *M.*
2 for a charity   ....
3 I'll tell you what ....
4 not very good   ....
5 get the idea   ....

Speaking and Listening 8

Talking about health

Speaking

1 🔊 63　**Choose the correct options. Then listen and check.**

1 **A** What's wrong with you?
  B I'm *boiling* / *exhausted*! I think I've got a temperature.

2 **A** What's the matter with you?
  B I feel *exhausted* / *terrifying*!

3 **A** You don't look very good!
  B I'm not! I've just got a *burn* / *cold* on my leg!

4 **A** You look awful!
  B And I *matter* / *feel* awful! I've got a headache and a bad cough.

5 **A** How do you feel?
  B I got up with terrible backache, but I'm feeling *not too good* / *a bit better* now.

2 🔊 64　**Complete the conversation with these phrases. Then listen and check.**

a bit better	~~Are you all right~~
drink some of this	How does it feel
sore throat	

A Hey! ¹*Are you all right*?
B No, I'm not. I've got a really ² ....
A How did you do that?
B I'm not sure. Maybe it was the concert last night.
A Hold on a minute. Here, ³ .... That should help you.
B Mmm! What is it?
A It's something my gran makes for colds and sore throats. ⁴ .... ?
B It tastes quite bitter!
A Yes, but what about your throat?
B Oh, that's ⁵ .... already, thanks.

Listening

3 🔊 65　**Listen and choose the correct options.**

1 Andy hurt himself *playing football* / *walking* .
2 He got back home by *ambulance* / *car*.
3 *Andy went to the doctor's.* / *The doctor visited Andy at home.*
4 Andy has to rest for ten *days* / *weeks*.
5 Trish suggests *going to the cinema* / *watching a film at home.*

4 🔊 65　**Listen again. Put these phrases in the order you hear them.**

a That was lucky!　　　....
b How did you get back?　....
c Why not?　　　　　....
d Not too good　　　.1..
e Poor you!　　　　....

Problems with machines

Speaking

1 🔊 **66** **Choose the correct options. Then listen and check.**

1 This digital recorder *isn't* / (*doesn't*) work.
2 I *can't* / *not* listen to the recordings I've made.
3 There might be *nothing* / *something* wrong with the battery.
4 Have you *check* / *checked* it?
5 Have you tried *press* / *pressing* the 'play' button?
6 You were pressing the *right* / *wrong* button!

2 🔊 **67** **Complete the conversation with these phrases. Then listen and check.**

Have you checked	~~Have you pressed~~
Let me have a look	something wrong
that doesn't work	I've tried that

A What's the matter?
B I can't change the channels on the TV.
A ¹*Have you pressed* the right button on the remote control?
B Yes, ² .... , but nothing happens and it was OK yesterday.
A Have you checked the volume control?
B Yes, and ³ .... either.
A Well, there must be ⁴ .... with the remote control then. ⁵ .... the batteries?
B Yes! I took them out and put them back in again.
A ⁶ .... Hmm, one of the batteries isn't making contact. Let's press it in better. There you are. Try it again.
B Yes, it works! Thanks!

Listening

3 🔊 **68** **Listen and choose the correct answers.**

1 The problem with the coffee maker was due to …
   a no electricity.
   b no coffee.
   c) no water.
2 The cause of the problem was …
   a a visitor.
   b a phone call.
   c a TV programme.
3 The problem lasted between …
   a five and ten minutes.
   b ten and fifteen minutes.
   c ten and twenty minutes.

4 🔊 **68** **Listen again. Put these phrases in the order you hear them.**

   a you're lucky   ....
   b that jug over there   ....
   c How did that happen?   ....
   d the red light on   .1..
   e That one!   ....

Pronunciation

Consonants

Symbol	Example	Your examples
/p/	park	
/b/	big	
/t/	toy	
/d/	dog	
/k/	car	
/g/	good	
/tʃ/	chair	
/dʒ/	jeans	
/f/	film	
/v/	visit	
/θ/	three	
/ð/	they	
/s/	swim	
/z/	zoo	
/ʃ/	shop	
/ʒ/	television	
/h/	hot	
/m/	map	
/n/	notes	
/ŋ/	sing	
/l/	laptop	
/r/	room	
/j/	yellow	
/w/	watch	

Vowels

Symbol	Example	Your examples
/ɪ/	rich	
/e/	egg	
/æ/	rat	
/ɒ/	job	
/ʌ/	fun	
/ʊ/	put	
/iː/	eat	
/eɪ/	grey	
/aɪ/	my	
/ɔɪ/	boy	
/uː/	boot	
/əʊ/	note	
/aʊ/	now	
/ɪə/	hear	
/eə/	hair	
/ɑː/	star	
/ɔː/	north	
/ʊə/	tour	
/ɜː/	world	
/i/	happy	
/ə/	river	
/u/	situation	

Pronunciation Practice

Unit 1 Sounds: /v/, /w/ and /b/

1 ◗) 69   **Listen and repeat.**

1 Can you drive the van along Avenue Five?
2 Will you wait for me while I'm away?
3 Meet Bill at the library, and bring your bicycle too!
4 Put the books in the bookcase and the bike on the balcony.
5 Put the heavy vases on the living room floor.
6 Where do you want to wait while they're away?

2 ◗) 69   **Put words from Exercise 1 in the correct columns. Then listen again and check.**

/v/	/w/	/b/
drive	will	Bill
....	....	....
....	....	....
....	....	....
....	....	....

Unit 2 Sentence stress

1 ◗) 70   **Listen and repeat the stressed words.**

1 What – do
2 What – do – work
3 What – doing
4 What – doing – morning
5 doing – homework – room
6 wasn't – games – laptop

2 ◗) 70   **Listen again and write the sentences.**

1 ....
2 ....
3 ....
4 ....
5 ....
6 ....

3 ◗) 70   **Listen again and repeat the complete sentences.**

Unit 3 /ɒ/ and /əʊ/

1 ◗) 71   **Listen and repeat.**

1 What a lot of shops!
2 I don't know!
3 What's he got in his pockets?
4 No mobile phones in here!
5 He lost his wallet in the forest.
6 Don't go home now!

2 ◗) 71   **Put words in Exercise 1 in the correct columns. Then listen again and check.**

/ɒ/	/əʊ/
what	don't
....	....
....	....
....	....
....	....

Unit 4 /ae/ and /ɑ:/

1 ◗) 72   **Listen and repeat.**

1 You can't charge your laptop batteries in the café!
2 Carry the backpacks please, Sam!
3 I'm having a dance party for passing the exam!
4 They ran into a traffic jam on the way to the match.
5 That's the first album she sang with the band.

2 ◗) 72   **Put words from Exercise 1 in the correct column. Then listen again and check.**

/ae/	/ɑ:/
laptop	can't
....	....
....	....
....	....
....	
....	

Pronunciation

Unit 5 /aɪ/ vs /ɪ/

1))) 73 **Listen and repeat.**

  1 There'll be bright sunshine in the five islands.
  2 The interactive visit begins at six.
  3 When I go by bike, I usually arrive on time.
  4 It's a pretty little village in Italy.

2))) 73 **Put words from Exercise 1 in the correct column. Then listen again and check.**

/aɪ/	/ɪ/
bright	interactive
....	....
....	....
....	....
	....

Unit 6 /ʌ/ and /juː/

1))) 74 **Listen and repeat.**

  1 Stewart cooks beautiful meals.
  2 There are tons of rubbish in the countryside.
  3 There's a long queue outside the new museum.
  4 I sometimes get money for running the washing machine on Sunday!

2))) 74 **Put words from Exercise 1 in the correct column. Then listen again and check.**

/ʌ/	/juː/
tons	beautiful
....	....
....	....
....	

Unit 7 *going to*

1))) 75 **Listen to the recording. <u>Underline</u> the sentences where you hear *gonna* instead of *going to*.**

  A What are you going to do today?
  B I'm going to join a demonstration.
  A What are you going to do?
  B I'm going to hold a placard and chant slogans.
  A Are you going to have lunch there?
  B I'm not going to make plans at the moment.

A Can you tell me what time you're going to come back?
B I dunno. I'm just going to take it easy.

2))) 75 **Listen again and repeat. First A, then B.**

Unit 8 *gh*

1))) 76 **Listen and repeat the sentences.**

  1 He caught eight fish and that was enough.
  2 They didn't laugh because they were frightened.
  3 She came home from holiday and brought a bad cough with her.
  4 They taught me that rough is the opposite of smooth.

2))) 76 **Put words from Exercise 1 with *gh* in the correct column. Then listen again and check.**

/f/	silent
enough	caught
....	....
....	....

Unit 9 /ɪ/ and /iː/

1))) 77 **Listen and repeat the sentences.**

  1 Please keep your feet off the table!
  2 It's a pretty little village in Italy.
  3 I'd like three kilos of green peas.
  4 If it isn't in the bin, then I can't think of where it is!

2))) 77 **Put words from Exercise 1 with the corresponding sounds in the correct column. Then listen again and check.**

/ɪ/	/iː/
It's	keep
....	....
....	....
....	....
....	....
....	....
....	....
....	

Irregular Verb List

Verb	Past Simple	Past Participle
be	was/were	been
become	became	become
begin	began	begun
break	broke	broken
bring	brought	brought
build	built	built
buy	bought	bought
can	could	been able
catch	caught	caught
choose	chose	chosen
come	came	come
cost	cost	cost
cut	cut	cut
do	did	done
draw	drew	drawn
drink	drank	drunk
drive	drove	driven
eat	ate	eaten
fall	fell	fallen
feed	fed	fed
feel	felt	felt
fight	fought	fought
find	found	found
fly	flew	flown
forget	forgot	forgotten
get	got	got
give	gave	given
go	went	gone/been
have	had	had
hear	heard	heard
hold	held	held
keep	kept	kept
know	knew	known
learn	learned/learnt	learned/learnt
leave	left	left
lend	lent	lent

Verb	Past Simple	Past Participle
light	lit	lit
lose	lost	lost
make	made	made
mean	meant	meant
meet	met	met
pay	paid	paid
put	put	put
read /riːd/	read /red/	read /red/
ride	rode	ridden
ring	rang	rung
run	ran	run
say	said	said
see	saw	seen
sell	sold	sold
send	sent	sent
shine	shone	shone
show	showed	shown
sing	sang	sung
sit	sat	sat
sleep	slept	slept
speak	spoke	spoken
spell	spelled/spelt	spelled/spelt
spend	spent	spent
stand	stood	stood
steal	stole	stolen
swim	swam	swum
take	took	taken
teach	taught	taught
tell	told	told
think	thought	thought
throw	threw	thrown
understand	understood	understood
wake	woke	woken
wear	wore	worn
win	won	won
write	wrote	written

My Assessment Profile Starter Unit

1 **What can I do? Tick (✓) the options in the table.**

⏪ = I need to study this again.　　⏸ = I'm not sure about this.　　▶ = I'm happy with this.　　⏩ = I do this very well.

		⏪	⏸	▶	⏩
Vocabulary (Student's Book pages 4–7)	• I can use common verbs correctly. • I can use prepositions correctly. • I can talk about everyday objects. • I can talk about school subjects. • I can talk about numbers and dates. • I can use opinion adjectives correctly.				
Reading (SB page 9)	• I can understand profiles on a school intranet page.				
Grammar (SB pages 4–7)	• I can use all forms of *to be* in the Present simple. • I can use all forms of *have got* in the Present simple. • I can use the possessive *'s* correctly. • I can tell the difference between different uses of the contraction *'s*. • I can use subject and object pronouns correctly. • I can use possessive adjectives correctly. • I can use indefinite pronouns correctly. • I can use the Present simple correctly. • I can use adverbs of frequency correctly. • I can use *was/were* correctly.				
Speaking (SB page 8)	• I can ask for and give personal information.				
Listening (SB page 8)	• I can understand conversations about personal information.				
Writing (SB page 9)	• I can write a personal profile.				

2 **What new words and expressions can I remember?**

words ....

expressions ....

3 **How can I practise other new words and expressions?**

record them on my MP3 player ☐　　　write them in a notebook ☐

test them with a friend ☐　　　translate them into my language ☐

4 **What English have I learned outside class?**

	words	expressions	
on the radio			
in songs			
in films			
on the internet			
on TV			
with friends			

My Assessment Profile Unit 1

1 What can I do? Tick (✓) the options in the table.

◀◀ = I need to study this again. ⏸ = I'm not sure about this. ▶ = I'm happy with this. ▶▶ = I do this very well.

		◀◀	⏸	▶	▶▶
Vocabulary (Student's Book pages 10 and 13)	• I can talk about rooms and parts of the house. • I can talk about furniture and household objects.				
Pronunciation (SB page 13)	• I can understand and say correctly the sounds /v/, /w/ and /b/.				
Reading (SB pages 11 and 16)	• I can understand articles about houses and rooms.				
Grammar (SB pages 12 and 15)	• I can use the Present simple and Present continuous correctly. • I can use verbs with the -ing form correctly.				
Speaking (SB pages 14 and 15)	• I can describe a place.				
Listening (SB page 16)	• I can understand people describing their homes.				
Writing (SB page 17)	• I can link similar and contrasting ideas. • I can write a description of a room.				

2 What new words and expressions can I remember?

words

....

expressions

....

3 How can I practise other new words and expressions?

record them on my MP3 player ☐   write them in a notebook ☐
test them with a friend ☐   translate them into my language ☐

4 What English have I learned outside class?

	words	expressions
on the radio		
in songs		
in films		
on the internet		
on TV		
with friends		

My Assessment Profile Unit 2

1   What can I do? Tick (✓) the options in the table.

⏪ = I need to study this again.   ⏸ = I'm not sure about this.   ▶ = I'm happy with this.   ⏩ = I do this very well.

		⏪	⏸	▶	⏩
Vocabulary (Student's Book pages 20 and 23)	• I can use adjectives to describe pictures. • I can use adjectives with prepositions.				
Pronunciation (SB page 23)	• I can hear stressed words in sentences and say sentences with the correct stress.				
Reading (SB pages 21 and 26)	• I can understand descriptions of pictures and stories behind the pictures.				
Grammar (SB pages 22, 23 and 25)	• I can use the Past simple and Past continuous correctly.				
Speaking (SB pages 24 and 25)	• I can ask for and give permission.				
Listening (SB page 26)	• I can understand people talking about photos.				
Writing (SB page 27)	• I can locate people and things in a picture. • I can write a description of a picture.				

2   What new words and expressions can I remember?

words

....

expressions

....

3   How can I practise other new words and expressions?

record them on my MP3 player ☐   write them in a notebook ☐
test them with a friend ☐   translate them into my language ☐

4   What English have I learned outside class?

	words	expressions	
on the radio			
in songs			
in films			
on the internet			
on TV			
with friends			

My Assessment Profile Unit 3

1   What can I do? Tick (✓) the options in the table.

◀◀ = I need to study this again.   ❚❚ = I'm not sure about this.   ▶ = I'm happy with this.   ▶▶ = I do this very well.

		◀◀	❚❚	▶	▶▶
Vocabulary (Student's Book pages 30 and 33)	• I can talk about shopping. • I can use shopping nouns and money verbs.				
Pronunciation (SB page 33)	• I can understand and say correctly the sounds /ɒ/ and /əʊ/.				
Reading (SB pages 31 and 36)	• I can understand articles about shopping.				
Grammar (SB pages 32 and 35)	• I can use comparatives and superlatives correctly. • I can use *too* and *enough* correctly. • I can use *much*, *many*, *a lot of* correctly.				
Speaking (SB pages 34 and 35)	• I can ask for help and respond.				
Listening (SB page 36)	• I can understand radio news reports.				
Writing (SB page 37)	• I can express my opinion in writing. • I can write a customer review.				

2   What new words and expressions can I remember?

words

....

expressions

....

3   How can I practise other new words and expressions?

record them on my MP3 player ☐   write them in a notebook ☐
test them with a friend ☐   translate them into my language ☐

4   What English have I learned outside class?

	words	expressions
on the radio		
in songs		
in films		
on the internet		
on TV		
with friends		

My Assessment Profile Unit 4

1   What can I do? Tick (✓) the options in the table.

⏪ = I need to study this again.   ⏸ = I'm not sure about this.   ▶ = I'm happy with this.   ⏩ = I do this very well.

		⏪	⏸	▶	⏩
Vocabulary (Student's Book pages 44 and 47)	• I can talk about news and the media. • I can use adverbs of manner.				
Pronunciation (SB page 47)	• I can understand and say correctly the sounds /æ/ and /ɑː/.				
Reading (SB pages 45 and 50)	• I can understand newspaper and magazine reports.				
Grammar (SB pages 46 and 49)	• I can use the Present perfect correctly. • I know when to use the Past perfect and when to use the Present simple.				
Speaking (SB pages 48 and 49)	• I can express doubt and disbelief.				
Listening (SB page 50)	• I can understand a recorded interview.				
Writing (SB page 51)	• I can check spelling, punctuation and grammar. • I can write a profile.				

2   What new words and expressions can I remember?

words

....

expressions

....

3   How can I practise other new words and expressions?

record them on my MP3 player ☐   write them in a notebook ☐

test them with a friend ☐   translate them into my language ☐

4   What English have I learned outside class?

	words	expressions	
on the radio			
in songs			
in films			
on the internet			
on TV			
with friends			

My Assessment Profile Unit 5

1   **What can I do? Tick (✓) the options in the table.**

⏪ = I need to study this again.   ⏸ = I'm not sure about this.   ▶ = I'm happy with this.   ⏩ = I do this very well.

		⏪	⏸	▶	⏩
Vocabulary (Student's Book pages 54 and 57)	• I can talk about holidays. • I know different meanings of the verb *get*.				
Pronunciation (SB page 56)	• I can understand and say correctly the sounds /aɪ/ and /ɪ/.				
Reading (SB pages 55 and 60)	• I can understand stories about travel experiences and tourist attractions.				
Grammar (SB pages 56 and 59)	• I can use the Present perfect with *for*, *since* and *just* correctly. • I can ask questions with *How long … ?*				
Speaking (SB pages 58 and 59)	• I can ask for information.				
Listening (SB page 60)	• I can understand information conversations.				
Writing (SB page 61)	• I can use adjectives and new vocabulary in my writing. • I can write a travel guide.				

2   **What new words and expressions can I remember?**

words

....

expressions

....

3   **How can I practise other new words and expressions?**

record them on my MP3 player ☐   write them in a notebook ☐
test them with a friend ☐   translate them into my language ☐

4   **What English have I learned outside class?**

	words	expressions
on the radio		
in songs		
in films		
on the internet		
on TV		
with friends		

My Assessment Profile Unit 6

1 What can I do? Tick (✓) the options in the table.

⏪ = I need to study this again.　　⏸ = I'm not sure about this.　　▶ = I'm happy with this.　　⏩ = I do this very well.

		⏪	⏸	▶	⏩
Vocabulary (Student's Book pages 64 and 67)	• I can talk about household chores. • I can use adjectives to describe feelings.				
Pronunciation (SB page 67)	• I can understand and say correctly the sounds /ʌ/ and /juː/.				
Reading (SB pages 65 and 70)	• I can understand articles about household chores.				
Grammar (SB pages 66, 67 and 69)	• I can use verbs to express obligation, no obligation and prohibition correctly. • I can make predictions with *will*, *won't* and *might*.				
Speaking (SB pages 68 and 69)	• I can give advice.				
Listening (SB page 70)	• I can understand conversations about problems and advice.				
Writing (SB page 71)	• I can explain reasons and results. • I can write a letter of advice.				

2 What new words and expressions can I remember?
words

....

expressions

....

3 How can I practise other new words and expressions?
record them on my MP3 player ☐　　write them in a notebook ☐

test them with a friend ☐　　translate them into my language ☐

4 What English have I learned outside class?

	words	expressions
on the radio		
in songs		
in films		
on the internet		
on TV		
with friends		

My Assessment Profile Unit 7

1 What can I do? Tick (✓) the options in the table.

⏪ = I need to study this again.　　⏸ = I'm not sure about this.　　▶ = I'm happy with this.　　⏩ = I do this very well.

		⏪	⏸	▶	⏩
Vocabulary (Student's Book pages 78 and 81)	• I can talk about protest and support. • I can use verbs with prepositions.				
Pronunciation (SB page 80)	• I can hear the difference between *gonna* and *going to*.				
Reading (SB pages 79 and 84)	• I can understand articles about protest and support issues.				
Grammar (SB pages 80, 81 and 83)	• I can use *be going to* and *will* correctly. • I can use the First conditional.				
Speaking (SB pages 82 and 83)	• I can persuade someone to do something.				
Listening (SB page 84)	• I can understand persuasion conversations.				
Writing (SB page 85)	• I can format a letter or email correctly. • I can write a formal letter.				

2 What new words and expressions can I remember?

words

....

expressions

....

3 How can I practise other new words and expressions?

record them on my MP3 player ☐　　write them in a notebook ☐

test them with a friend ☐　　translate them into my language ☐

4 What English have I learned outside class?

	words	expressions
on the radio		
in songs		
in films		
on the internet		
on TV		
with friends		

My Assessment Profile Unit 8

1 What can I do? Tick (✓) the options in the table.

⏪ = I need to study this again.　　⏸ = I'm not sure about this.　　▶ = I'm happy with this.　　⏩ = I do this very well.

		⏪	⏸	▶	⏩
Vocabulary (Student's Book pages 88 and 91)	• I can use extreme adjectives. • I can talk about illness and injury.				
Pronunciation (SB page 91)	• I can hear the difference between *gh* with the sound /f/ and silent *gh*.				
Reading (SB pages 89 and 94)	• I can understand articles about danger and risk.				
Grammar (SB pages 90 and 93)	• I can use the Second conditional correctly. • I can use relative pronouns.				
Speaking (SB pages 92 and 93)	• I can talk about health.				
Listening (SB page 94)	• I can understand conversations about accidents and health.				
Writing (SB page 95)	• I can interpret an application form. • I can fill in an application form correctly.				

2 What new words and expressions can I remember?

words

....

expressions

....

3 How can I practise other new words and expressions?

record them on my MP3 player ☐　　write them in a notebook ☐

test them with a friend ☐　　translate them into my language ☐

4 What English have I learned outside class?

	words	expressions
on the radio		
in songs		
in films		
on the internet		
on TV		
with friends		

My Assessment Profile Unit 9

1 What can I do? Tick (✓) the options in the table.

⏪ = I need to study this again.   ⏸ = I'm not sure about this.   ▶ = I'm happy with this.   ⏩ = I do this very well.

		⏪	⏸	▶	⏩
Vocabulary (Student's Book pages 98 and 101)	• I can talk about machines. • I can use machine related nouns and verbs.				
Pronunciation (SB page 101)	• I can understand and say correctly the sounds /ɪ/ and /iː/.				
Reading (SB pages 99 and 104)	• I can understand articles about machines and inventions.				
Grammar (SB pages 100 and 103)	• I can use the Present simple passive and Past simple passive correctly. • I know when to use *by* in passive sentences.				
Speaking (SB page 104)	• I can talk about problems with machines.				
Listening (SB pages 102 and 103)	• I can understand conversations about problems with machines.				
Writing (SB page 105)	• I can organise an opinion essay. • I can write an opinion essay with reasons and examples.				

2 What new words and expressions can I remember?

words

....

expressions

....

3 How can I practise other new words and expressions?

record them on my MP3 player ☐   write them in a notebook ☐
test them with a friend ☐   translate them into my language ☐

4 What English have I learned outside class?

	words	expressions
on the radio		
in songs		
in films		
on the internet		
on TV		
with friends		

Pearson Education Limited,
Edinburgh Gate, Harlow
Essex, CM20 2JE, England
and Associated Companies throughout the world

www.pearsonelt.com

© Pearson Education Limited 2013
The right of Joe McKenna to be identified as author of
this work has been asserted by him in accordance with the
Copyright, Designs and Patents Act, 1988.

First published 2013
Thirteenth impression 2024

ISBN 978-1-4479-4363-1

Set in 10.5/12.5pt LTC Helvetica Neue Light
Printed in Slovakia by Neografia

Acknowledgements

The publisher would like to thank the following for their kind permission
to reproduce their photographs:

(Key: b-bottom; c-centre; l-left; r-right; t-top)

Alamy Images: allesalltag 106/5, Andre Seale 83, Archimage 25t, Arco
Images GmbH 40, Ashley Cooper 69, blickwinkel 17b, Christine Nichols
17c, Cliff Hide News 119, Colin Underhill 106/2, 110/1, Colin Underhill
106/2,110/1, Gallo Images 55, Ian Dagnall 82c, Mark Boulton 110/4,
Matthew Chattle 108/3, Mode Images 50, NielsVK77, Nikolay
Mihalchenko 109/4, Plinthpics 106/1, redsnapper 121, Ron Bull 106/3,
Stephen Dorey ABIPP 115, SuperStock 25b, Tony Watson 113, vario
images GmbH & Co.K 45, way out west photography 108/2, Young-
Wolff Photography 35t; **Bridgeman Art Library Ltd**: The Yellow House,
1888 (oil on canvas), Gogh, Vincent van (1853-90) / Van Gogh Museum,
Amsterdam, The Netherlands 48; **Corbis**: Bob Krist 114, Monty
Rakusen / cultura 105/3, Nancy Honey / cultura 112/5; **Fotolia.com**:
126-135, withGod 35b; FotoLibra: Mkimages 104/5, Nicola Mary
Barranger 109/3; **Getty Images**: Alistair Berg / Digital Vision 109/5, Art
Wolfe / Stone 110/2, Bernard Jaubert / StockImage 17t, Britt Erlanson /
The Image Bank 105/5, Ghislain & Marie David de Lossy / Cultura
108/4, Jae Rew / Stockbyte 30, John Howard / Lifesize 109/2, Larry
Dale Gordon / The Image Bank 120, Maria Teijeiro / Lifesize 23, Paul
Burns / Digital Vision 105/4, Javier Pierini / Taxi 56; **Pearson Education
Ltd**: Gareth Boden 80; **Press Association Images**: Brynjar Gauti / AP
22, Leanne Italie / AP 66, Stefan Rousseau / PA Archive 110/5; **Rex
Features**: DI CROLLALANZA / SIPA 41, Image Broker 82t, Ray Tang
106/4, View Pictures 9; **Science Photo Library Ltd**: SINCLAIR
STAMMERS 108/5; **Shutterstock.com**: alanf 49, Alex Yeung 14, Anton
Gvozdikov 73, Bambuh 111/3, Stacy Barnett 111/5, Blend Images
111/1, CandyBox Images 109/1, Edw 118, Francois Étienne du Plessis
107/5, hansenn 74, Heidi Schneider 105/2, Hung Chung Chih 110/3,
Kitch Bain 104/2, Kokhanchikov 104/1, Lance Bellers 108/1,
michaeljung 43, Monkey Business Images 13t, 61, Monkey Business
Images 13t, 61, oksana2010 111/4, Olena Zaskochenko 13b, photobar
107/4, Photoseeker 104/3, Rechitan Sorin 104/4, tristan tan 117, Yuri
Arcurs 112/4; **SuperStock**: Scott Stulberg 105/1, Zefa 78; **The Kobal
Collection**: UNIVERSAL PICTURES 116; **Veer/Corbis**: Adrian Britton
112/1, JohnKwan 112/2, Petr Malyshev 82b, Roman Ivaschenko 112/3,
smithore 111/2

All other images © Pearson Education

Cover image: *Front:* **Shutterstock.com**: Corepics VOF

Every effort has been made to trace the copyright holders and we
apologise in advance for any unintentional omissions. We would be
pleased to insert the appropriate acknowledgement in any subsequent
edition of this publication.

Illustrated by: Moreno Chiacchiera pages 4, 5, 8, 11, 15, 34;
Peskimo pages 10, 24, 39, 50, 60, 65, 107; Paula Franco pages 19, 27,
29, 47, 63, 71, 73.